# PRE-ARYAN
## AND
# PRE-DRAVIDIAN IN INDIA

# PRE-ARYAN
## AND
# PRE-DRAVIDIAN IN INDIA

SYLVAIN LEVI
JEAN PRZYLUSKI
JULES BLOCH

TRANSLATED FROM FRENCH BY

**PRABODH CHANDRA BAGCHI**

GYAN

*Published by*

GYAN

Gyan Publishing House
5, Ansari Road
Daryaganj, New Delhi-110002
Phone: 011-47034999, 9811692060
E-mail: books@gyanbooks.com

*Distribution Network*
gyanbooks.com
India, USA, Canada, UK, Australia, France



ISBN : 978-81-212-3915-8 (PB)
First Published, Calcutta, 1929

2nd Impression 2020

*Printed at:* Gyan Press, Delhi.

# PRE-ARYAN AND PRE-DRAVIDIAN IN INDIA

BY

SYLVAIN LÉVI, JEAN PRZYLUSKI
and JULES BLOCH

Translated from French
by
PRABODH CHANDRA BAGCHI, M.A. (Calcutta),
D.-ès-Lettres (Paris),
Lecturer in the University of Calcutta

PUBLISHED BY THE
UNIVERSITY OF CALCUTTA
1929

# PREFACE

As the following articles have opened up a new field of enquiry, I have found it necessary to make them accessible to our scholars and students. I am thankful to the authors, Professors Sylvain Lévi, Jules Bloch and Jean Przyluski, for kindly permitting me to publish these translations in the form of a book. The introduction is meant for our students, and it does not pretend to be exhaustive. A number of similarities between Indo-Aryan and Austric words have been suggested by my friend and colleague Dr. S. K. Chatterji, and such suggestions have also occurred to me. As some of the words noted by us are popular vernacular terms, not usually registered in dictionaries, it was thought that their discussion might be *à propos* to the subject so brilliantly inaugurated by the eminent French scholars.

In spite of my best endeavours, some possible slips in translation and transliteration, have crept in: for these I crave the indulgence of the authors as well as the reader. But these, I hope, will not detract from the merit of the original papers, which are singularly valuable for the reconstruction of the foundations of our history and culture.

I have gratefully to acknowledge the assistance I received from Dr. A. C. Woolner for having gone through portions of the translation in MS., and also from Dr. S. K. Chatterji for his constant active interest in the publication of the work.

P. C. BAGCHI.

THE UNIVERSITY,
CALCUTTA :
*1st May, 1929.*

# TABLE OF CONTENTS

# INTRODUCTION.[1]

## Austro-Asiatic.

A linguistic unity in the Mon-Khmer group (then called Mon-Annam) was first pointed out by Logan and others and established on a sure footing by Keane in 1880. Forbes in his work, *Comparative Grammar of the Languages of Further India* (1881), incontestably proved the existence of this linguistic unity. In 1888 Müller[2] continued the same study further. Kuhn in 1889 while emphasising on this linguistic unity remarked[3] "what is more striking is the relation with Annamite; there is undeniable relation of the monosyllabic group: Khasi-Mon-Khmer with Kolh, Nancowry, and the dialects of the aborigines of Malacca."

Schmidt pushed the work of Kuhn further[4] and established the relation between the languages of the Malay peninsula and the Mon-Khmer group. He studied also the correspondence in the vocabularies[5] and the phonetic laws of those languages. He then applied these laws to

[1] The first part of the Introduction is based on (and partly translated from) the French translation of Pater Schmidt's article. *Cf.* BEFEO VII, pp. 217ff.

[2] *Grundriss der Sprachwissenschaft*, Vol. IV (Appendix).

[3] *Beiträge zur Sprachen-kunde Hinterindiens*, Sitz. der K. bayer Akad-der wissensch. phil. hist. KL 1889, I, p. 219.

[4] *Die Sprachen der Sakei und Semang auf Malakka und ihr Verhältnis zu den Mon-khmer Sprachen*, Bijdragen tot de Taal—Landen Volkenkunde van Nederl. Indië, 6th series, Part VIII.

[5] *Grundzüge einer Lautlehre der Mon-khmer Sprachen* (1905), Denkschriften der Kaiserl. Akad. d. Wiss. in Wien (phil. hist.), KL, Vol VIII,

the study of Khasi.[1] In an appendix to his study of Khasi he examined Palong, Wa and Riang of the middle valley of the Salween. Palong was already connected with the Mon-Khmer family by Logan and Kuhn. Grierson in his *Linguistic Survey* (II, pp. 1, 38ff.) added Wa and Riang to it. Wa and Riang extends almost to the same latitude as Khasi.

Schmidt next studied [2] the Nikobarese and by a study of its phonology proved that it belongs to the Mon-Khmer family and is related to other languages which belong to the same group. There is resemblance even in particular details of vocalism and consonantism. It has the same development for the roots in *ya* and *wa* as in the Mon-Khmer languages, the same for the mode of the production of palatals. As to the morphology, it presents some earlier phases of morphological development in many cases and gives us the key for explaining a series of forms in Mon-Khmer.[3] Nicobarese is not pollysyllabic as often said; the roots are monosyllabic like other Mon-Khmer languages and are developed by infixes and prefixes. There are besides suffixes in it which are completely missing in other Mon-Khmer languages. Most of these suffixes indicate direction (as it happens in the languages of islands) meaning cardinal points. But there are a few which have purely grammatical function. Hence Nikobarese is a link between the Muṇḍā (or Kol) and the great

[1] *Grundzüge einer Lautlehre der Khasi-Sprache in ihren Beziehungen zu derjenigen der Mon-khmer Sprachen* (1905): Abhandlungen der kõnigl. Bayer Akad. d. Wiss. (I. KL, Vol. XXII, III).

[2] *Cf. Gr. Mon-khmer Sprachen*, §§ 199 ff. and 225 ff., *Gr. Khasi-Sprache*, § 151ff.

[3] *Cf.* Appendix to *Die Mon-khmer Võlker, ein Bindeglied Zwischen Võlkern Zentralasiens und Austronesiens*, 1906 (*cf.* French Translation, BEFEO, VII, pp. 251ff.).

Austronesian group which also possess suffixes besides prefixes and infixes.

Sten Konow (*Linguistic Survey*, IV, p. 11) established the relation between the Muṇḍā and the Mon-Khmer groups on phonological grounds. " Both families possess," he says, " aspirated hard and soft letters. Both avoid beginning a word with more than one consonant. The most characteristic feature in Muṇḍā phonology are the so-called semi-consonants: *k'*, *ch'*, *t'*, *p'*. They are formed in the mouth in the same way as the corresponding hard consonants *k*, *ch*, *t*, *p*, but the sound is checked and the breath does not touch the organs of speech in passing out. The sound often makes the impression of being nasalised and we therefore find writings, such as *tn*, or *dn* instead of *t'*; *pm*, or *bm* instead of *p'*; and so forth. Some corresponding sounds exist in Sakei and connected languages. In the Mon-Khmer forms of speech final consonants are, as a general rule, shortened in various ways. Similarly in Cham final *k*, *t*, *p*, *h* are not pronounced and their enunciation is at last checked so that only a good observer can decide which sound is intended." As to the formation of words in both the groups Sten Konow noticed only a few characteristics, but it was Schmidt again who proved that the system of the formation of words with the help of prefixes and infixes is identical in both the groups.

In these two groups of languages (Muṇḍā and other Mon-Khmer groups) all consonants that they possess with the exception of *ṅ*, *ñ*, *y*, and *w* can serve as simple prefixes, and, as in the most of the Mon-Khmer languages, a second degree of prefixation by insertion of a nasal (*ṅ*, *ñ*, *m*, *n*) or a liquid (*r* [ *l* ?]) between the prefix and the root may take place. Some of the infixes used are identical in both the families as regards their form as well as their function.

The infix *n* forms names of instruments in the Mon-Khmer and abstract nouns which designate the result of an action in the Muṇḍā languages. The forms of the last category are not however rare in Khmer, Bahnar and Nikobarese, and inversely the Muṇḍā languages have names of instruments formed by the infixation of *n*. The infix *p* forms abstract words in Santali. The same phenomenon is observed in Khmer, but only in the root words of which the initial is *y*, *r* or *l*, whereas for words beginning with other initials the double infix *mn* is found. There is another remarkable point of resemblance between Nikobarese and Muṇḍā: the latter forms a kind of superlative by inserting *p* and the former a comparative by *n*, but in both the cases we are in the presence of abstract words and mannerisms analogous to the expression: *he is goodness itself*.

Besides the infixes and prefixes the Muṇḍā languages also make use of suffixes. On this point they do not agree with Mon-Khmer and Khasi but with Nikobarese. The formation of some intransitives, passives and substantives corresponds precisely with Santali *ok'*, *ak'*, Muṇḍāri *o*, and Kūrkū *u* which are used in the formation of passives, reflexives, and intransitives. Besides the adjectival suffix *o* in Nikobarese seems to be identical with the suffix *ao* of Santali which forms verbs of condition. The large quantity of other suffixes which have made the Muṇḍā conjugation a complex one is not found in Nikobarese and still less in Khasi and Mon-Khmer (the last two having no suffixes). But this does not go against the theory of relationship between the two groups of languages. It is the necessary consequence of another unique and important difference.

It consists in the fact that Muṇḍā uses the genitive (without affix) before and Mon-Khmer, Khasi, and

Nikobarese after. A law [1] has been established that the languages which have the genitive before the word governed (without affix) are languages possessing suffixes, while those which have the genitive coming after are languages possessing prefixes. This law is to be applied here. The fact that the Muṇḍā presents such a rich development of suffixation is due to its position of genitive being before the word. Since the establishment of this law the attention has been drawn to the importance of possessive affixes which have preserved, for a very long time, the ancient position of the genitive. The case is similar with Muṇḍā. In forms like *apu-n'* "my father," *apu-m* "your father," etc., the genitive which is placed before in other cases has been placed after in those cases; because *apu-ń* is nothing but *apu-ań* "father (of) mine." This proves that the Muṇḍā languages, in ancient times, had postposition of genitive and it is from that time onwards that their system of prefixes, which exist now in a state of survival, has come down. The present anteposition of genitive has been introduced through the influence of Dravidian, Aryan, or Tibeto-Burman languages which surrounded the Muṇḍā domain and have actually penetrated into it. Thus the most serious difficulty in connecting the two groups of languages is gone. A large concordance between the two vocabularies supports it. Schmidt has shown that Santali has about 500 words (reduced to about 350 roots) in common with Mon-Khmer, Khasi, and Nikobarese.[2]

Schmidt has thus proved the relation of the Muṇḍā languages with Nikobarese, Khasi and Mon-Khmer

[1] *Cf.* Schmidt's lecture to the Vienna Anthropological Societ published in *Völker psychologie* of Wundt, Vol. I, *cf.* also Mitteilur des Anthrop. Gesselschaft in Wien, XXXIII, pp. 381-389.

[2] *Cf.* Appendix referred to in note 3; pii.

and established the existence of a linguistic family called by him **Austro-Asiatic**. It comprises, according to him, the following groups :

I. *Mixed Group* : Čam, Radé, Jaraï, Sedang, which are Mon-Khmer judged by their construction and vocabulary but has borrowed a large number of words, even personal pronouns and words for numbers.[1]

II. *Mon-Khmer* : the two ancient literary languages, Mon and Khmer, Bahnar, Stieng, dialects of the tribes called Moï : Samreh, Kha-so, Kha Tampuen, Schong, Huei, Suc, Sue, Hin, Nahhang, Mi, Khmus, Lemet, all in Indo-China ; and in the peninsula of Malaya, Bersisi and Jakun.[2]

III. *Senoi* (*Sakei*)-*Semang* in Malacca.[3]

IV. *Palong-Wa-Riang*.[4]

V. *Khasi*.[5]

VI. *Nikobarese*.

VII. *Muṇḍā* : or *Kol* the two sub-groups, the more eastern *Kherwari* with Santali, Muṇḍāri, Bhumij, Birhoṛ, Koḍā, Ho, Turi, Asuri, and Korwa dialects, and the western Kūrkū ; Khaṛiā ; Juang ; and the two mixed languages, Savara and Gadaba.[6]

The Muṇḍā languages occupy the eastern half of Central India. Dravidian is on its south and penetrates

[1] *Dictionnaire Čam-français* by Aymonier and Cabaton, Paris, 1906 (*cf. Anthropos*, II, pp. 330-332).

[2] Khmer texts published by Abbot Guesdon, *Anthropos* I, pp. 91-92, *Bahnar Grammar* and *Dictionary* by Dourisboure (Hongkong 1889), *Stieng Dictionary* by Azimar (Paris 1887 not complete).

[3] Skeat and Blagden : *Pagan Races of the Malay Peninsula*, (*cf.* Vocabulary), London 1906, *Anthropos*, II, pp. 598, 604.

[4] *Linguistic Survey of India*, II.

[5] *Ibid*, II, pp. 17-57. *An Anglo-Khasi Dictionary* by H. Roberts (1878).

[6] *Linguistic Survey of India*, IV (1906), pp. 1-275.

it at several points. It has been now definitely proved that there is no relation between the two groups. On the southern border of the Himalayas Sten Konow has found out some languages, which though of Tibeto-Burman origin, present some characteristics similar to those in Muṇḍā. There we find, no doubt, the last traces of the Muṇḍā which once existed in that region. The westernmost of these dialects is the Kanawari in the valley of the Sutlej spoken at the confluence of the Sutlej and the Spiti, *i.e.*, the southern frontier of Kashmir. To the east, in Nepal, Kanāṣī, Mancāṭī, Ranglōī, Bunan, Raṅkas, Dārmiyā, Caudāṅsī, Byāṅsī, and Dhīmal are connected with it. It should be therefore admitted that the domain of Muṇḍā, Mon-Khmer and other connected languages was much more considerable than it is at present. It is only in later times that this domain has been reduced and cut into pieces by Aryan and Dravidian on the west and Tibeto-Burman on the east.

The seven linguistic groups, enumerated before, can be reduced to three principal groups according to Schmidt. Santali (or Muṇḍā in general) is more closely related to Mon-Khmer than to Khasi. Nikobarese occupies a middle position between Khasi (and Wa languages) and Mon-Khmer-cum-Muṇḍā. Berisi (and Jakun) of Malaya is more related to the latter group than to the Senoi-Semang as expected from its geographical position. On the contrary a division must be established in the second group: Semang, Tembe, Senoi, and Sakei.[1] The Semang dialects should be put apart and the Senoi (Sakei, Tembe) should be considered as a particular group by itself. Both may be included in a more general group but it should be pointed out that Senoi inclines more towards the Berisi

[1] *Die sprachen der Sakei und Semang ant Malakka und ihr verhältnis zu den Mon-khmer Sprachen*, p. 135.

dialects (and consequently to the Mon-Khmer) and probably presents a mixture of those dialects with Semang. Regarding the last it should be pointed out that the words by which it differs from other languages of Malaya and from Mon-Khmer have not yet been identified. It is besides probable that there are in them the vestiges of the original language of the Semang-Negritos, now lost. It becomes more certain when we consider the cases in which the Mon-Khmer languages agree primarily between themselves. In such cases it appears to be less and less probable that these words of the Semang language come from a particular group of the great family of Mon-Khmer-Muṇḍā-Nikobar-Khasi languages. The case is similar with the word "bird"; Semang has a particular root *kauau* while other languages have another root *sim*; for "child" Mon-Khmer-Muṇḍā-Nikobar-Khasi, etc., have the root *kwan* while Semang has *wañ*; for "hand" Semang has *ćas* while others have *tai*, *ti*.

Lastly a study of some ancient loans from Aryan throws some light on the classification of these languages. Three of these loans are interesting. (1) Sanskrit *jaṅghā* is found under the forms *gaṅga*, *gañ*, *joñ*, *jöñ*, *jüñ*, *ioñ*, etc., in Santali, Wa, Palong, Riang, Mon-Khmer, Senoi, Berisi and Jakun but is missing in Nikobarese, Khasi, Semang and the other Muṇḍā languages. (2) Sanskrit *salākā* seems to be missing in Muṇḍā and Nikobarese. In Semang there are *hali*, *hale*, etc., which are a little doubtful on account of the secondary forms: *kli* and *klit*. Everywhere else we have *saluka*, *slak*, *slik*, *sla*, *hla*, *la*. (3) Sanskrit (*u*)*daka* is found everywhere under the forms *dak*, *ḍāk*, *dik*, *dok*, etc[1]., except in Khasi, Wa, Palong, Riang, Semang and probably Senoi. Only

[1] The above is Pater Schmidt's view. But it may be questioned if the Austric words are at all derived from Indo-Aryan.—P. C. B.

the Mon-Khmer (and Muṇḍā) possess these three loan words; on the contrary the three other groups possess one and Semang probably none. It can therefore be concluded that the last three groups represent the most ancient stage in development and have preserved for these three concepts the ancient roots, which Mon-Khmer and Muṇḍā possessed originally but—(and it is important for determining the period of migration of the different groups towards their present abode) which they lost after their more prolonged and intimate commerce with their Aryan neighbours.

The following classification necessarily follows from the explanation given above:

I. (*a*) Semang;
   (*b*) Senoi (Sakei, Tembe); for their mixture with Berisi, *cf.* III(c).

II. (*a*) Khasi;
   (*b*) Nikobarese;
   (*c*) Wa, Palong, Riang related to Mon-Khmer (*cf.* IIIa);

III. (*a*) Mon-Khmer (with Bahnar, Stieng, etc.);
   (*b*) Muṇḍā or Kol;
   (*c*) Čam, Radé, etc., mixed with Austronesian languages.

### Austro-Asiatic and Austric.

Schmidt has extended his studies even further and proposed to connect the Austro-Asiatic[1] family with Austronesian which consists of several well-determined

[1] Prof. Przyluski has criticised this nomenclature (see p. 149, n. 2 of this book) and has proposed some modifications.

groups: Melanesian, Polynesian, Micronesian and Indonesian.[1] He has studied these two large groups and discovered in them the following common features: (1) Absolute similarity in the phonetic system, (2) a complete basic unity in the structure of words, (3) several important and characteristic features in the grammar, *viz.*, the postposition of the genitive; affixation and partially the form of the possessive; the presence of an exclusive and inclusive form for the first person plural of the personal pronoun in some of these languages; the existence of a dual and a trial in some of these languages; (4) large agreement in vocabulary.

On these grounds Schmidt proposed to establish a larger linguistic unity between Austro-Asiatic and Austronesian and called[2] the family thus constituted "**Austric.**" M. Rivet wants to extend this family even further and included in it the languages spoken in the Oceanic group, *i.e.*, Australian,[3] Papuan, and Tasmanian.[4]

[1] *Die Mon-Khmer Völker, ein Bindeglied zwischen Völkern Zentralasiens und Austronesiens*, 1906 (French translation: *Les Peuples Mon-Khmèrs, trait d'union entre les peuples de l'Asie centrale et de l'Austronesie*, BEFEO, VII, pp. 213-263, VIII, pp. 1-35).

[2] *Le Group océanien, Bull. Soc. Ling.*, 1926 (83), pp. 141-168.

[3] Schmidt already suggested it in his study on *Die Gliederung der australischen Sprachen*, *Anthropos*, Vols. VII, VIII, IX, XII, XIII.

[4] Prof. Przyluski (cf. *infra*, p. 147) has raised the problem of the relation between *Sumerian* and *Austro-Asiatic*. He has compared a series of Austro-Asiatic words with Sumerian and has discovered important analogies. M. Rivet also in his article already referred to suggests that the Sumerians had probably played an important role as agents of transmission of cultural elements between Oceania and Europe and Africa. But it would be premature, as Prof. Przyluski himself admits (*infra*, p. 148), to give any verdict at the present moment.

### Austro-Asiatic and Indo-Aryan.

While Prof. Thomsen maintained that a Muṇḍā[1] influence has probably been at play in fixing the principle regulating the inflexion of nouns in Indo-Aryan vernaculars, such influence appeared to be unimportant to Prof. Sten Konow. He found it more probable that the Dravidian languages had modified Aryan grammar in such characteristics and the Muṇḍā family had thus, at the utmost, exercised but an indirect influence through the Dravidian forms of speech. He, however, admitted that some phenomena of Bihari, like the conjugation of verbs, the use of different forms to denote an honorific or non-honorific subject or object and the curious change of verb when the object is a pronoun of the second person singular can be conveniently explained as due to Muṇḍā influence.

Recent studies have tried to establish that this influence can be traced further back. Prof. Przyluski in his papers, translated here, have tried to explain a certain number of words of the Sanskrit vocabulary as fairly ancient loans from the Austro-Asiatic family of languages. He has in this opened up a new line of enquiry. Prof. Jules Bloch in his article on *Sanskrit and Dravidian*, also translated in this volume, has criticised the position of those

[1] Dr. S. K. Chatterji prefers to call the Muṇḍā family *Kōl*, as the word *Kōl*, according to him, is (in the Sanskrit-Prakrit form *Kolla*) an early Aryan modification of an old Muṇḍā word meaning "man" (*The Study of Kōl*, *Calcutta Review*, 1923, p. 455). Prof. Przyluski also accepts his explanation (*infra*, pp. 28-29). As the word *Muṇḍā* has the disadvantage of being the name of special group of this family (*viz.*, the tribe which centres round the city of Ranchi in Chota Nagpore and whose language is called *Mundari*), it would perhaps be better to adopt the word *Kōl* for the common designation of this particular branch of the Austro-Asiatic race or speech.

who stand exclusively for Dravidian influence and has proved that the question of the Muṇḍā substratum in Indo-Aryan cannot be overlooked.

But the problem has other aspects too, and it has been further proved that not only linguistic but certain cultural and political facts also of the ancient history of India can be explained by admitting an Austro-Asiatic element. In 1923, Prof. Lévi, in a fundamental article on *Pré-Aryen et Pré-Dravidien dans l'Inde* tried to show that some geographical names of ancient India like *Kosala-Tosala, Aṅga-Vaṅga, Kaliṅga-Triliṅga, Utkala-Mekala* and *Pulinda-Kulinda*, ethnic names which go by pairs, can be explained by the morphological system of the Austro-Asiatic languages. Names like *Accha-Vaccha, Takkola-Kakkola* belong to the same category. He concluded his long study with the following observation: "We must know whether the legends, the religion and the philosophical thought of India do not owe anything to this past. India has been too exclusively examined from the Indo-European standpoint. It ought to be remembered that India is a great maritime country... the movement which carried the Indian colonisation towards the Far East...was far from inaugurating a new route...Adventurers, traffickers and missionaries profited by the technical progress of navigation and followed under better conditions of comfort and efficiency, the way traced from time immemorial, by the mariners of another race, whom Aryan or Aryanised India despised as savages." In 1926, Przyluski tried to explain the name of an ancient people of the Punjab, the *Udumbara*, in a similar way and affiliate it to the Austro-Asiatic group. (Cf. *Journal Asiatique*, 1926, I, pp. 1-25, *Un ancien peuple du Pendjab—les Udumbaras*: only a portion of this article containing linguistic discussions has been translated in the Appendix of this book.) In another article, the same scholar discussed some names of Indian towns in the geography of Ptolemy and tried to explain them by Austro-Asiatic forms.[1]

In another series of articles, Prof. Przyluski is trying to prove a certain number of Indian myths by the Austro-Asiatic influence. He studied the Mahābhārata story of Matsyagandhā and some legends of the *nāgī* in Indian literature, compared them with similar tales in the Austro-Asiatic domain and concluded that " these stories and legends were conceived in societies living near the sea, societies of which the civilisation and social organisation were different from those of the neighbouring peoples : the Chinese and the Indo-Aryans." (Cf. *La princesse à l'odeur de poisson et la nāgī dans les traditions de l'Asie orientale*, Études Asiatiques, II, pp. 265-284. Prof. Przyluski continued the same study in another article *Le Prologue-cadre des Mille et une Nuits et le Thème du Svayaṁvara, Journal Asiatique*, 1924, ccv, pp. 101-137.)

Coming to modern languages of India also Prof. Przyluski has arrived at interesting results. He has contributed two articles on this subject, one of which on the *Bengali Numeration and Non-Aryan Substratum* has been translated in this book (pp. 25-32). In this article he has traced the origin of the Bengali *kuḍi* (twenty) to the Austro-Asiatic domain. In another article on *the Vigesimal Numeration in India*[2] he tries to determine the

[1] *Bull. de la Société de Ling*. 1926 (28), pp. 218-219; *infra*, pp. 136-148; we must admit that the conclusions of Prof. Przyluski are not convincing.

[2] *La numération vig ésimale dans l'Inde* published in the *Rocznik Orjentalistyczny*, T. IV (1926), pp. 230-237. It reached me too late to be translated in this collection. Its summary is given below.

origin of the numeration by twenties. Having proved in his former article that the notion of twenty is really based on the human body, he points out that, as a man possesses four members, each provided with 5 fingers, 5 = hands, and 20 = man, are higher composite units in the Austro-Asiatic numeration. 5 and 20 having the same relation to each other as 1 to 4, the next higher number which could be quite naturally conceived was 80 bearing the same relation to 20 as 20 has to 5. It would be interesting to note in this connection the affinities of the Bengali word *pan* or *pon* = one anna = 4 pice = 80 cowrie shells = 80 pieces in computing for instance betel leaves or straw bundles. In Santali *pon* or *pan* means 80 (Campbell, *Santali Dictionary*, s.v. *pon*); cf. *bar pon gachi* "160 bundles of rice-seedlings" in which *bar* means 2 and *pon*, 80. The origin of the word *pon* = 80 can be easily determined if we observe that in Santali *pon* means also 4. *Pon* or *pan* is certainly used for 4 (twenties). Eighty (*i.e.*, four twenty) being the tetrade *par excellence* ended by being shortened into "four." *Pon* or *pan* thus plays in Santali the same role as 100 in ours. It is a composite unit and the highest of all. The habit of counting by tetrades and twenties, once introduced, *pon*, *i.e.*, 80 could be considered as the agregate of 20 tetrades. This way of counting is usual in Santali in which *pon*, *pan* = 80 is said to be formed of 20 *goṇḍa* or *gaṇḍa* : *gaṇḍa* means a group of 4, *i.e.*, tetrade.

| *gaṇḍa* | *kuḍi* | *pon* |
|---|---|---|
| 4 | 5 × 4 = 20 | 20 × 4 = 80 |

In this operation 4 seems to have taken a capital interest. This is probably why *gaṇḍa* not only means the inferior tetrade of 4 but also the action of division. Thus we have:

*pon gaṇḍa*=4 tetrades =16

and *gaṇḍa guṇḍa* "fragments, to be broken in pieces, to be reduced to powder."

*gaṇḍa guṭi* "to divide, to count."

(*Cf.* A. Campbell, *A Santali English Dictionary*, s.v. *gaṇḍa guṭi*: "the system of *gaṇḍa guṭi* is to put down a pebble or any other small object, as the name of each person entitled to share is mentioned. Then a share is placed alongside of each pebble, or whatever else was laid down.)"

It is possible to show that this system has been known not only to the people speaking the modern Indo-Aryan languages but also to Sanskrit. Amongst the meanings attributed to the word *gaṇḍaka* (St. Petersburg Dictionary) we have "*c*) division, separation, a certain way of counting, a system of counting by 4 (*cf.* Bengali *gaṇḍā*=4); a money equal to 4 *kaṇḍis*."

As the Skt. word *gaṇḍaka* means a coin equal to 4 cauris it has a greater chance of being a loan from the Austro-Asiatic languages. First of all the word has the same meaning as that of Santali *gaṇḍa*; besides the use of cauri shells (*cypraea moneta*) as a money is not an Indo-European custom. It is the characteristic of a maritime civilisation which was developed on the shores of Indian Ocean and the China Sea, *i.e.*, the region where the people speaking the Austro-Asiatic languages were disseminated. In the 13th century this money was in current use in Bengal. The series containing the multiples of cauri is marked by the frequency of the tetrades and the use of the factor four. The table of their values are still preserved:

| | | |
|---|---|---|
| 4 *kauṛi* | = | 1 *gaṇḍā* |
| 20 *gaṇḍā* | = | 1 *paṇ* or 80 *kauṛi* |
| 4 *paṇ* | = | 1 *āna* |
| 4 *āna* | = | 1 *kāhan* or ¼ of a rupee approximately (cf. *Hobson-Jobson*, s. v. cowry). |

It is possible to connect with modern Indo-Aryan *paṇ* the Santali numeral *pan* or *pon* meaning 80, and such is its numerical value in the system:

1 *paṇ* = 80 *kauṛi*.

*Paṇa* is besides a Sanskrit word and the Sanskrit vocabulary *Trikāṇḍaśeṣa*, III, 3, 206 teaches us that 20 cauris = ¼ *paṇa*. *Paṇa* in Sanskrit has therefore the same value as *pan* = 80 in Santali.

On the whole, the three tetrades at the basis of the Muṇḍā numeration,—*ganḍa* = 4, *kuri* = 4 × 5 = 20, *pan* = 4 × 20 = 80—are enumerated in the same way in Bengali and Santali and the words *gaṇḍa(ka)* and *paṇ(a)* belong also to the Sanskrit vocabulary. These analogies can be explained only by loans from Muṇḍā. In contact of maritime populations who used cauri and counted by twenties, some Indo-Aryan groups have adopted the Austro-Asiatic monetary unit and the vigesimal numeration;[1] these foreign words have also introduced in their vocabulary along with it.

Prof. Przyluski has proposed to continue further his interesting study on numeration.

This is all that has been done till now on the Austro-Asiatic substratum and loans in Indo-Aryan. The results, already arrived at, are sufficient to draw our attention

[1] Counting by twenties is still current amongst some lower castes of Bengal.—P. C. B.

to this new field of investigation. Besides the studies already noticed we have to refer to the work of J. Hornell [1] who admits a strong Polynesian influence on the Pre-Dravidian population of the Southern coast of India. He thinks that a wave of Malayan immigration must have arrived later, after the entrance of the Dravidians on the scene, and it was a Malayan people who brought from the Malay Archipelago the cultivation of the coco-palm. Besides, in a few papers contributed to the Journal of the Asiatic Society of Bengal, Prof. Das Gupta has brought out the striking analogy between some sedentary games of India (specially of the Central Provinces, Bengal, Bihar, Orissa and the Punjab) and those of Sumatra.[2]

Finally Dr. J. H. Hutton, in an interesting lecture on the *Stone Age Cult of Assam* delivered in the Indian Museum at Calcutta in 1928, while dealing with some prehistoric monoliths of Dimapur, near Manipur, says [3] that "the method of erection of these monoliths is very

[1] *The Origins and the Ethnological Significance of the Indian Boat* designs (A. S. B. Memoir, Vol. VII, 1920).

[2] *A Few Types of Indian Sedentary Games*, etc., J.A.S.B. XXII (1926), pp. 143-148, and 211-213. It will be noticed that the names of some of these games end in the word *guṭi* (*do-guṭi*, *tre-guṭi*, *nao-guṭi*, *bara-guṭi* prevalent in the Punjab) which as Prof. Das Gupta says, means, "pieces." The word is evidently the same as Santali *guṭi* (of *ganḍa guṭi* noticed before by Prof. Przyluski). The word has the chance of belonging to the Austro-Asiatic vocabulary.

[3] Cf. *Man in India VIII* (1928), No. 4, pp. 228-232. About the celts or stone adzes and axes discovered in Assam he says that "it was probably hafted in the Polynesian manner between two layers of wood lashed together. By far the commonest type is a slightly shouldered type, derived from the Irrawaddy or Mon-Khmer. Mon-Khmer forms also survive in language and folklore throughout Assam. The adze type is found in the Ganges Valley, but was probably brought by the emigrants from the east."

important, as it throws some light on the erection of prehistoric monoliths in other parts of the world. Assam and Madagascar are the only remaining parts of the world where the practice of erecting rough stones still continues,...The origin of this stone cult is uncertain, but it appears that it is to be mainly imputed to the Mon-Khmer intrusion from the east." In his opinion the erection of these monoliths takes the form of the *lingam* and *yoni*. He thinks that the Tantrik form of worship, so prevalent in Assam, is probably due to "the incorporation into Hinduism of a fertility cult which preceded it as the religion of the country. The dolmens possibly suggest distribution from South India, but if so, the probable course was across the Bay of Bengal and then back again westward from further Asia. Possibly the origin was from Indonesia whence apparently the use of *supari* (areca nut) spread to India as well as the Pacific." [1]

[1] I have not been able to consult the recent publication of M. Nobuhiro Matsumoto, *Le Japonais et les langues Austroasiatiques*, in which he appears to have opened another new line of Austro-Asiatic research.

# I[1]

## [S. K. C.]

# SOME MORE AUSTRIC WORDS IN INDO-ARYAN.

(READ BEFORE THE FIFTH ALL-INDIA ORIENTAL CONFERENCE, LAHORE, NOVEMBER, 1928.)

A new and a most important line of investigation has been inaugurated by Dr. Jean Przyluski by his researches into the philology of the Austric element in our Indian Aryan speeches, beginning from Sanskrit downwards. The presence in the Indo-Aryan speeches of a considerable number of Austric words (allied, it would seem, more to the Mon-Khmer than to the Kol or Munda group) is of very great significance in the study of the origins of the Hindu people and Hindu culture of Northern India. These words demonstrate borrowing from Austric dialects at a time when they were spoken by masses of people, evidently on the Gangetic plains. The people who spoke these Austric dialects have now merged into the Hindu (or Mohammedan) masses of Northern India: they have become transformed into the present-day Aryan-speaking castes and groups of the country. The words indicate the kind of objects, ideas, and institutions which persisted and which the Aryan world had to adopt in

[1] All references like [A 80(b)], [B 353-354] in the following notes are to the vocabulary of Skeat and Blagden. The letter represents that of the vocabulary under it. The names of the languages and dialects as well as of authorities and sources are given in abbreviated form after each word within brackets.

howsoever modified a form. M. Przyluski in his very valuable papers to the *Mémoires de la Société de Linguistique de Paris* and in the *Journal Asiatique* has indicated the line of his enquiries and his methods, and has given his derivations of a number of Sanskrit words which are borrowings from the extinct Austric dialects current in Northern India. The corresponding forms in the speeches related to Mon and Khmer, and to Khasi, namely, the various Austric languages of Indo-China, Malaya and in some cases of the islands of Indonesia, also have been carefully collated by M. Przyluski, and their etymology as Austric forms, which can only be satisfactorily explained as being built up with Austric roots and affixes, has been given. He has made a very good case that words like *liṅga, lāṅgula. kambala, tāmbūla, kadali*. etc., are from the Austric, and are not Aryan words. The valuable and indispensable *Comparative Vocabulary of Aboriginal Dialects* of the Malay Peninsula, in Vol. II of Skeat and Blagden's *Pagan Races of the Malay Peninsula* (London, Macmillan & Co., 1906) is a repository of words from the Austric speeches of the forest tribes (Sakai, Semang, etc.) of British Malaya, and it also contains cognate forms in Mon, Khmer and other Indo-Chinese Austric speeches, Khasi and Nicobarese as well as in the Austric dialects of Malaya and Indonesia and the Kol speeches of India. Dr. P. C. Bagchi has suggested affiliating a further batch of words in Indo-Aryan to Austric and it was from a study of this comparative vocabulary that a number of obvious agreements with Indian forms and words presented themselves to him. I have also been studying this vocabulary with very great interest and profit, and a few similarities, which may or may not be fortuitous or accidental, have struck me also—similarities between some of our unexplained or unsatisfactorily explained words in Sanskrit and in other Indo-Aryan speeches, and words and roots in the Austric languages as noted by Blagden and Skeat. These I am tempted to record below for what they are worth.

Anger, angry : Assamese *khaṅga* (খঙ্গ), Bengali khā̃khār (খাঁখার) abuse, punishment, khā̃khā̃ (খাঁখাঁ, in খাঁখাঁ ক'রে ওঠা to get furious). *Cf.* kheŋ, khiŋ (Khmer), tĕ-kēñ (Jak. Mad.), tĕkeng (Jak. ; Jak. Ba. ; Pa.) ; tĕken (Jak. Sim). [A 80(b).]

Bow, arrow : Skt. *bāṇa, pināka* ; *bāṇa* has been already treated by Przyluski (*cf. infra*, p. 19). For *pināka* (=pin+āka) *cf.* ig ?, āg (Semang), ak (Stieng), āk (Riang), anak (Malay), etc. [B 353-354].

Bamboo : Bengali, bā̃khārī (বাঁখারী), *bākhārī* (বাখারী) =split bamboo. *Cf.* iré ( Sak. Ra. ) ? ; karek, tarek, =to split, to divide, in Mon : *e.g.* tun (dun) kărek =split bamboo. For 'bamboo' the common words are lĕbuih, lĕbeh (Semang dialects) ; buloh (Malay) ; pô-o' (Sem. Cliff.) ; poo' (pook), pau, (pauk) (Serau) ; pō' (pok) (Sak.). The Bengali bā̃khārī-*bākhārī* may be either from a compound like *pok-karek >*bok-karek, or from bā̃ś <*vaṃśa*+karek >bā̃h-karek. [B 21, 22, 35.]

Bat : Bengali *bāduḍ* (বাদুড়) =**bad*+affix-*uḍa* -*ḍa*. *Cf.* hāpēt, sāpēt (Bes. Sep. A. I.), hompet (Bes. Songs.), samet, hamet (Bahnar), kawet, kowet (Sem. Stev.), kāwed, kauid (Sem. Pa., Max., Sem. Bukb., Max.), kawät, ganät (Sem. K. Ken), kät (Kaseng), kawa <*kawat (Mon) ; not (Stieng) ; wåt-da, wāt-da, wåt (Andamanese). [B 74, 76].

Bird : Hindi cīḍiyā, (चिँड़िया) =*cī-ḍ-iā*. *Cf.* cäm, cem (in some Sakai and Semang dialects) ; ka-cim (Mon) ; cim (Cham) ; kcim (Charē), sem (Bahnar) ; sim (Palaung) ; sim=cock (Santali). Also cä*m*ṛä (Santali, Mahle, Muṇḍāri, etc.). [B 216].

Breast (Female) : Skt. *cucuka* : *cf.* Malay susu, milk : may be onomatopoeic. [ B 387].

Charcoal : Skt. *aṅgār*, Hindi *iṅgel* : *cf.* anggu (Sem. Jur. New); jeng-kâ, jengkat (Sak.), nying-kah (Sen.); embers : engong ōš, ingung us, etc. (Sem.); Firewood : api (Jak.); Fire logs : anggeng (Bes.); burning embers : răngök (Khmer). [C 77.]

Cheek : Skt. *kapōla* : *cf.* kĕbang (Sem. Pa. etc.); kapå (Sak.); Face : kapō, kapau (Sak.); tapōa (Nicobar, Central and South); Cheek : thpeal < thbāl (Khmer). The Skt. word may be Austric in origin—ka-pōla, pola representing the original root. [C 81] Compare *kapāla* head, Bengali কপাল *kapāla*=forehead, which has been suggested as " Oceanian " by P. Rivet, 'Le group Océanian,' MSL., 1927, p. 149.

Coconut : Skt. *nārikela* : *cf.* Malay niyor (coconut), niyor (Sak. and Sem.); fruit : ple, phlei, etc., kolai (Tareng); (*cf. infra*, p. 54), kölai (Kontu); *nārikela* may be derived from equivalents of niyor (coconut) and kolai (fruit), combined. [C 197 ; F 282.]

Cloth : Bengali *kāni* ( কানি ) meaning a rag. *Cf.* Malay kain.

Crab : Skt. *kamaṭha*, *karkaṭa*, Bengali *kāṭhā* ( কাঠা ), keṭe ( কেটে ) < kāṭhiā : *cf.* kătam (Malay); khatām (Mon), kedam, ktam (Khmer); kötam (Bahnar); tam (Stieng); kat-kom (Santali). [C 258.]

Female : Oriya *māikiniā* ( माइकिनिआ ), Oriya *māipa* (माइप); *cf.* kena, kna (Sak., Sem.); kinnah (-handsome woman), mai-könah (Or., Berumb.); miniah (Sem., Klap.); măbä (Sem. Kedah); wife, woman=mabe (Sem., Stev.), mabä (Sem.). [F 62, 64, 65.]

Frog : Skt. *bheka*. *Cf.* tabek, tabeg (Sạkai), buāk (Malay) [F 268]. [Toad in some Bengali dialects is *bhāuā beṅg* ( ভাউয়া বেঙ )—*cf.* buā' in Mandr. Malacc.—P. C. B.]

Foot : Skt. *jaṅghā*, Bengali *jāṅ* ( জাঁং ) : *cf.* chan chong, jöng, jaung ; jukn (Sem., Sak.) ; jöng (Mon) ; jung (Stieng) ; jöng, cöng (Khmer) ; jan (Palaung) ; jangga (Santali). [F 220.] [Schmidt thinks the word is a Sanskrit loan in Austric.]

Heel : Beng. *goḍāli* ( গোড়ালি ) : *cf.* duldul (Sem.) ; düöl, ka-duol (Cham) ; ken-töla, lah (Central Nicobar). But Bengali ( গোড় ) *gōḍ*=foot, Prakrit *goḍḍa* are to be noted. [H 69.]

Leech : Skt. *jalūkā, jalaukā*. *Cf.* jĕlô (Sen.), jhlöng (Khmer) ; glu (Stieng, Chrau). [L 46.] (Uhlenbeck suggests an Indo-European origin in his " Etymologisches Wörterbuch.")

Leg (calf of leg) : Bengali *ṭheṅg* ( ঠেং ), *ṭeṅgrī* ( টেংরী ) means the part of the leg between heel and calf. *Cf.* the words for leg : kĕteng (Sem. Kedah, Sem. Jarum) ; part from knee to ankle : skting (săkĕting), tin (Sem. Buk. Mak.) ; leg=k'teng, k'taing (Selung) ; kĕting (Malay). [C 6.]

Lip (Lower) : Beng *ṭhōṭ* ( ঠোঁট ), Skt. *tuṇḍa*. *Cf.* tĕnud (Sem.) ; Snout of animals—tnud (Sem.) ; mouth—thno (Khmer). [N 203.] But see *infra* p. 56.

Mad : Beng. *pāgal* (পাগল) : *cf.* gila (Malay) ; gilā, gilā' (Sakai). [M 3].

Mosquito : Skt. *maśaka*, Hindustani *macchaḍ* ( মচ্ছড় ) ; *cf.* kâmet, kâmos, kumus (Sakai) ; kemit (Senoi) ; gamit (Mon) ; mūs (Khmer) ; moe (Stieng) ; sömec (Bahnar). (Uhlenbeck regards it as Indo-European, comparing Lithuanian 'masalâi,' Russian 'mosoliti,' etc.) [M 180].

Moustache : Bengali *moch* ( মোচ ), usually derived from Old Indo-Aryan *śmaśru* > Prakrit *mhacchu, mhaṁsu* ; but *cf.* misei, bisai (Sak.) ; misai (Semang) ; misai (Malay) ; But *cf. infra* p. 56. [M 198.]

Mud : Prakrit *cikkhilla*, Old Bengali *cikhila* ( চিখিল ), Hindustani *kīcaḍ* ( कीचड़ ) : *cf.* cica' (Sem.). [M 215.]

Mustard : Skt. *sarṣapa* = Pkt. *sāsava*, which remains unexplained. But *cf.* Malay sĕsawi. (The Malay word may be a Prakrit borrowing ; but it is Skt., and not Pkt., which furnishes Aryan loans in Indonesian.) [M 231.]

Musty, tainted : Bengali *bāsi* ( বাসি ) = kept overnight, unwashed : *cf.* Malay basi. [M 232.]

Neck : Bengali *ghāḍ*, ( ঘাড় ), Middle Bengali *ghāṭā* ( ঘাটা ) ; *cf.* ngot, ngod (Semang), gloh (Sak) ; gullet, throat = gälo (Sak.). *Cf.* Skt. *gala*, Bengali *galā*, ( গলা ) ; [N 23, 28.]

Rat : Skt. *indura, undura* ; *cf.* kândŏr (Khmer) ; kon (Old Khmer). [R 33].

Rattan : lataik (Semang) ; Khmer loda = climbing rattan ; can these be connected with Skt. *latā* ? [R 36.]

Rice (husked) : Skt. *taṇḍula*, Beng. *cāül* ( চাউল ) Middle Bengali ( তাঁড়ুল ) tā̃ṛula, ( তাউল ) *tāula*, ( চাউল ) *cāula*, *cf.* cĕngrong, cĕn-er-oi, ceng-goi, ng-roi (Sakai) ; also Sakai cendaroi, cendroi ; cendaroi (Senoi); jaroi, caroi (Sak.) cooked rice : caroi (Sak.), srō (Mon), srauv (Khmer). [R 112].

Roof : Bengali chā̃c ( ছাঁচ ) = thatch ; chā̃c-talā ( ছাঁচ-তলা ) = eaves, *chon̄cā* ( ছোঁকা ) in East Bengal (Jessore, Dacca); *cf.* Semang cencâm, cin-com. [R 164].

Shell-lime : Bengali *kali cūn* ( কলিচুণ ) : *cf.* kālo (Sak.) ; kalāk (Sem.). [S 151].

Small : Beng *choṭo* ( ছোট ) : *cf.* eset (Sem.), cŏt (Bes.), kasut (Sem.) ; bạcit, macut, ma'cut, macât, măcŏt ; măjot, măcet, etc. (Sakai) ; cut (Achinese) ; asit (Cham); taăiet (Bahnar) ; [S 282]

Spleen : Skt. *plīhā* ; Uhlenbeck explains it as Indo-European, <*spelγhā ; but *cf.* kĕm-pil, kĕm-pal (Semang). [S 393].

Stomach, belly : Bengali *peṭ* ( পেট ), Prakrit *poṭṭa* ; *cf.* lĕpoch (U. Cher.) ; lĕpot (Serting) ; lopot (U. Ind.) lĕpu (Bera). [B 164.]

Skin disease: Old Beng. *kacchu* ( কচ্ছু ), Modern Bengali *khos* ( খোস ) ; *cf.* gas, gach (Sak., Sem.) ; gach, gai (Bahnar, =scab of animal). [I 46.]

White : biug (Sen.) ; biȧg, ḅiok (Sak.) ; biäg (Sem.) ; bōk (Stieng) ; bak (Bahnar) ; pu, bụ (Mon) ; can these be connected with Skt. *baka, vaka,* a bird which is white ? *Cf.* Assamese *bagā,* Panjabi *baggī* white. [W 98.]

Wood : Bengali *jhop* ( ঝোপ ), *jhoṛ* ( ঝোড় ), *jhāṛ* ( ঝাড় ) ; *cf.* jahu' (Sem.) ; jehūp chu (Mon) ; chö (Khmer) ; etc. Tree=jehū, jihu (Sak.). [T 211.]

## II

## [ P. C. B. ]

Skt. *ghaṇṭā*=bell ; *cf.* the word for a kind of drum gentang (Sak. Kor. Gb) ; gĕndang (Malay) ; rentak (Bes. Songs.). [D 175-176.]

Beng. ( তু ) *tu* or ( তু-তু ) *tu-tu*=special call for attracting a dog ; see also the Jaina *Ācārāṅga sūtra* (Tr. Jacobi, SBE XXII, p. 84) : "Mahāvīra travelled in the pathless country of the Lâḍhas, in Vajjabhûmi, Subbhabhûmi...many natives attacked him. Few people kept off the attacking, biting dogs. Striking the monk they cried *khukkhû* (=*chucchû*) and made the dogs bite him." The word *chu-chû,* which has remained unexplained, seems to be no other than a word for 'dog.' The region mentioned, Lâḍha (Râḍha), Subbhabbûmi (Suhma), etc., is still partly occupied by the Kol people who speak an Austric language. In Bengal while calling a dog the word *cu* or *cucu* (more commonly *tu* or *tutu*) is used.

*Cf.* the Austric words for dog : chhke (Khmer), chükè (Kon Tu), cho (tcho), etc. (in Old Khmer, Sedang), chò (Annam, Suè, Halang, Boloven, Sedang), chŏ (Kaseng), shŏ (Churu), achŏ (Tareng), chiōk ? chû, (Sem.), chuâ (Söm), chüuä, chuo, chuō, chu-o' (Sak.), etc. The Skt. *kukkura* would seem to be of different origin (=<**kurkura*). [D 143.]

Bengali *coṅgā* (চোঙ্গা, চোঙ) : spoon : *cf.* coŋ-keh (Bes. A. I.) ; coŋkhe (Bes. K. L.) ; congkhe' (Bes. Songs) Paddle—pĕnuŋkä ; to scoop up—coŋkoh. [S 398.]

Beng. *meḍā* (মেড়া)—"Sheep ;" *cf.* the word for 'goat' in the Kol family. mārām kō, merom kū (Santali, Mahle, Muṇḍāri, Birhor, Korwa, Khaṛia, etc.) *Linguistic Survey*, IV, n. 152 ; Bengali *bheḍā* meaning a sheep may be connected with the same word.

Skt. *gaja*—elephant : *cf.* the word for elephant gaui, gago (U-Kel) ; gaja (Sem. Beg.) ; gājāh (Tembi) ; gazah, gadjah, gajeh (Sem.) etc. ; kasōt (Sak. Kor. Gb.) : gôsêl (Bland); the word for rhinoceros in Sak. Sel. Da,—gu-sil—probably belongs to the same group. [E 51.]

Skt. *gaṇḍāra*—'rhinoceros'; the other word for rhinoceros in Skt.—*khaḍga* literally meaning 'a kind of broad sword' is certainly derived from its weapon of defence. Can the word *gaṇḍāra* be connected with another group of words for elephant ? gantir (Ben. New.), gĕntúl (Kena. I), gĕntäl (Bendu II), sogāntēl (Pant. Kap. Log.), sêgântū (Jak. Sim.). [E. 51.]

Skt. *kapota*—literally means a 'pigeon' but also used in the general sense of bird. *Cf.* the word for bird kăwōd (*pr.* kō-wōdd) (Sem.), kawod (Sem. Plus), kawot (U Pat.), kawau, kāwau etc. [B 215.]

Skt. *kāka*—crow [Bengali Semi-tatsama = *kāg*, tadbhava = *kāuā* কাউআ ; *cf.* Chatterji, *Origin, etc., of Bengali*

*Language*, I, p. 320]. *Cf.* the words for crow, gagak (Mal.), wŭkăg (Sem. Pa. Max), aag (Tembi), gaag (Seran), gaăk (Sem. Buk. Max.), daak (Ben. New); da'ak (Bes. A. I.), agăg (Sem. Skeat.); kaèk (Khmer), àk (Annam), ăk (Bahnar), âk (Boloven), ak (Jarai), khăḍăk (Mon.) etc. [C 277].

Bengali *boāl* (বোয়াল), Late Skt. *vaḍāla*=a kind of big fish with teeth : *cf.* the words for 'crocodile'—buaya (Mal), bayul (? Pang. U. Aring); bayul (Pang. Sam.), baul (U. Kel.), bayah (Sem.), baya, bajul (Java.), etc. [C 270.] Can the Skt. word for crocodile, *kumbhīra*, Pkt. *kumbhīla*, be connected with this group?

Skt. *halāhala*=poison : *cf.* the Austric word for snake (cobra)—hāle-(hali) (Sem. Buk. Max); jekop halek (Pang. U. Aring); ekob pĕlai ? (aikub plăi) (Sem. Buk. Max). [S 318.]

Bengali *karāt* ( করাত )=saw (**kara-vāta* <MIA *kara-vatta*, OIA *karapatra*, Maraṭhi, Gujrati *karvat*, Hindi *karaut*, *karot*: Chatterji, *op. cit.*, p. 336). But the Skt. form *karapatra* may be a Sanskritised form of the Austric words for 'cutting,' 'chopping,' etc.: kĕrat (Malay), kĕrat (Jak. Malac.), krat (grat) (Sak. Kor. Gb.), ya-krod (pr. krodd) (Pang. Gal.); to clear a jungle—krat (Kena. Stev.). [C 295, 301.]

Bengali *dā* ( দা ), *dāo* ( দাও )=Skt. *dātra*, chopper: on this word, Chatterji (*op. cit.*, p. 255, n. 1) adds the note—" দা - 'dā' is explained by Grierson as being from a form '*drāta' attested from Kāśmīrī ; it is found in Hindi as '*dāw*, *dāū*,' bill, sickle, and the occurrence in Skt. of the forms '*dāti*,' sickle, scythe, '*dāta*,' mown, cut off, '*dātṛ*' -mowing, mower, shows that the source of the NIA word is not '*dātra*' but rather some form like '*dātṛ*' (although the Kōl word '*datrom*' sickle, evidently an old Aryan borrowing, would show that '*dātra*' was quite a popular OIA vocable)." But may we not connect it with another series of Austric words for "cutting"?—*Cf.* tăt (Mon), tăh (Stieng), tieh, tih (Kaseng), toït (Bes. Malac.), töyt (Bes. Sep. A. I.), töyt (Mal.), katoyt (Bes. Sep. A. I.), tiet (Boloven), töh (Khmer). [C 297.] *Cf.* Burmese dah.

Skt. *vātiṁgaṇa*, *vātigaṇa*, Bengali bāïgaṇ, begun (বাইগণ, বেগুন) = brinjal. *Cf.* the Austric words for brinjal: tiong, tiung, ting, etc., in different Semang dialects. The word for fruit in the same language is bāh, bāho, bōh, etc. Skt. *vātiṁgaṇa* or *vātigaṇa* might be derived from a group bāh + tiong. [S 339, F 284.]

Skt. *dāḍimba*, *kadamba*, *śimba*, *nimba*, *rambhā*, *lābu*, *alābu*, *nimbu(ka)*, *jambu*, *jambura*, Bengali *nebu* or *lebu* *jāmb(h)īra*, *jāmīr*, etc., this whole series may belong to the same group. The last parts of the above words, all of which are names of fruits seem to represent the Austric word for fruit already noted in the case of *vātiṁgaṇa*. The variants of this word in different Semang and Sakei dialect, are: bāh, buh, bōh, buah, *cf.* F 284. There are indeed in these languages names of fruits in which bāh, buh, etc., form a part. *Cf.* banana = buah suguh; coconut = bûah pûlau; pomegranate = bāh dĕlimā (bah dlima) *cf.* F 284, B 179. Of the series mentioned, *lābu* and *alābu* have been already treated by M. Przyluski (*infra* p. 155ff.). If we start with the word for fruit 'bah, buh' we can explain the words in the series by prefixes like *k*, *t*, *r*, *l*, *j*, etc.—prefixes admitted in the formation of Austric words,—and the nasal infix. In *kadamba* a second degree of prefixation is visible—*ka* + *ta* + *m* + *ba*, and in *jambura*, a suffix, *-ra*. Skt. *ḍimba* = egg may belong to the same series. The word for egg in Sakei (Sel. Da) is *woat*. *Cf.* also Skt. *stamba*, *tumba*, *tumburu*, and also *udumbara* treated by Przyluski (*infra* p. 149).

Skt. *guḍa*=molasses; *cf.* the Austric words for 'sugar': gúla (Sak. Tap.); gula (Söm); gulã (Sak. Kerb.); gūla (Darat); hūlö (Jelai); gula (Malay). [S 512.]

Beng. *pagār* (পগার) meaning 'a water channel' 'ditch,' for raising a sort of obstruction (*cf.* Skt. *prākāra*; Bengali *gaḍ* (গড়) is used in the same sense. *Cf.* the Austric words for fence: pagar (Sak. U. Kam.); pagar (Mal.), pagar (Santali). In Santali *pagrao* means 'to construct a water channel' (see A. Campbell—*Santali-English Dictionary*). *Cf.* also Przyluski *infra* pp. 143-144.

# INTRODUCTION

PART I

# NON-ARYAN LOANS IN INDO-ARYAN

BY

JEAN PRZYLUSKI

# Non-Aryan Loans in Indo-Aryan

## I[1]

In India the people speaking the Aryan languages, have been in contact with those who speak other languages since ancient times. Besides the Dravidian languages, which apparently have no affinity with other linguistic groups, we find in the north the mass of Tibeto-Burmese languages and in the east the scattered islets of Thai, Mon-Khmer, and Muṇḍā. The Tibeto-Burmese family is generally connected with the Chinese and the Thai languages. The Muṇḍā (or Kōl) languages, on the contrary, are related, through the intermediary of Khasi, to Mon-Khmer and the dialects of the Malaya Peninsula. It has even been recently affirmed that this southern group of Mon-Khmer, Khasi, Muṇḍā, etc., must be connected with the Sino-Tibetan group (Conrady in *Aufsätze zur-Kultur und Sprachgeschichte vornehmlich des Orients, Ernst Kuhn Gewidmet*..., pp. 475-504), but it is a hypothesis yet and not a proved fact. In the following articles, I would call the *ensemble* of the Muṇḍā, Khasi, Mon-Khmer and Annamite languages as

[1] This article first appeared in 1921 in *Memoires de la Socie'te' de Linguistique de Paris* XXII, 5, pp. 205-208. Since then the progress in my research has compelled me to modify it.

the "Austro-Asiatic family" according to the terminology of Father Schmidt. It will be frequently necessary for me to consider the Indonesian languages also in this connection as they have very great affinities with the above family.

When the Aryans came from the temperate regions and spread over tropical India, they had no word in their vocabulary for a large number of plants, animals and unknown products of the new country. Thus it can be supposed *a priori* that they acquired important loans from the languages of the non-Dravidian populations with whom they first came into contact. I propose to show that such was really the case. Instead of trying to multiply proofs of *rapprochements*, I shall confine myself here to some typical examples ; I may however come back to the examination of this question subsequently, with more developments.

## Sanskrit *kadalī*

Skeat and Blagden have already classified all the names of "banana" occurring in the languages of Malaya Peninsula and the languages related to them. I will reproduce § B-42 of their admirable comparative vocabulary :

Banana, plantain : kĕlui ? (gelúi ; or glui), *Sak. Kor. Gb* ; tĕluwi or kĕluwi. *Sem. Jarum* ; tĕlūi. *Sem. Kedah* ; (telui). *Sak. Br. Low* ; (telonille) [? misprint for telouille]. *Sem. Ken.* ; (*tölouï*), *Söm* ; (*tölouï*), *Sak. Kerb.* ; ( tlouï), *Sak. Croix* ; telui, teloi. *Tembi* ; telei, *Serau* ; telēï, *Jelai* ; teli, telai, *Darat* ; telī, *Sak. Em.*; telū, *Sem. Per.*; tĕlāy. *Sak. U. Kam* ; tĕlai. *Tan. U. Lang* ; tlāi, tlāy. *Sak. U. Bert* ; tlai. *Sak. Sung* ; tĕ-lê. *Sen. Cliff* ; klē, *Sak, Blanj. Sw* ; (spec. *Mal.* pisang mas) telei mas, *Serau* ; (species unidentified), telui puntuk ; telui Jeleï [*i.e.*, of Jelai],

*Tembi* [*Southern Nicobar* talūi, "plantain"; *Khmer* tut taloi (tout taloi), "banana tree" (*tut* appears to mean "tree"); *Palaung* kloai "plantain"].

All these forms present a root with initial *l* provided with a complex vocalic element in which *i* generally appears. This root is preceded by a prefix sometimes syllabic *ke-*, *ge-*, *ta-*, *tö-*, *te-*, sometimes reduced to *k-*, *g-*, *t-*. It is probable that, amongst the syllabic forms of this prefix, *ke-*, *tö-*, *te-* are already reduced forms of **ka-*, **ta-*, which are more archaic and are often found in the Austro-Asiatic languages. On the other hand, it appears that the root originally possessed a long *ī* which had been converted into diphthongs in different ways. We can, therefore, restore two ancient forms of the name of banana: **ka-lī* and **ta-lī*.

We have in Sanskrit *kadalī* and *kandalī*, both of which mean banana or the banana tree. These forms, inexplicable in Indo-European, can be explained if we start from **ka-lī*. It seems that a simple infix *-da-* in *ka-da-lī* and a double infix *-n-da-* in *-ka-n-da-lī* have been inserted between the prefix and the root. The existence of infixes, *-d(a)-* and *-n-d(a)-* have been already recognised in the Austro-Asiatic languages, but their role is still undefined. I shall show later on, that they have actually entered, into some of the names of trees, like the "cabbage palm."

Besides *kadalī* and *kandalī* there had been doubtless, a third form **tandalī* in Indo-Aryan. In fact one of the eight kinds of syrup allowed by the Buddha to the monks is the *cocapāna*. According to the commentary of the Mahāvagga, VI, 35, 6, *coca* would be a kind of *kadalī*, and *cocapāna* would mean plantain syrup. Now Yi-tsing in *Ekaçatakarman*, VI, explains *coca* by *tan-da-li* (*A Record of the Buddhist Religion*, translated by J. *Takakusu*, p. 125, n. 1, and p. 220). *Tandalī* can be explained by starting from *ta-lī* in the same way as *kandalī* from *ka-lī*.

SANSKRIT *bāla-*, *kambala-*, *śimbala-*.

Amongst the words which mean the hair of men and animals in the languages of the Far East one may quote :

| | | | |
|---|---|---|---|
| Malay | *bulu* | Batak, Dayak | *bulu* |
| Čam | *balau* | Dagal | *polok* |
| Jaraï | *bölāu* | Malagasi | *volo.*[1] |

The same root explains some names for "cotton" in the Indo-Chinese languages :

| | | | |
|---|---|---|---|
| Jaraï | *köpal* | Annamite | *vai* |
| Sek | *köpal* | Laotian | *fāy.* |

In Jaraï and Sek, the root is preceded by the prefix *kö*. In Annamite and Laotian the final liquid is changed to *y*, as it occurs frequently in the Austro-Asiatic languages.

For the origin of these forms we can, therefore, suppose a root **bala-*, **bulu* meaning "hair, wool." We have in Sanskrit *bāla-*, *vāla-*, *vāra* which have the same sense. The word is ancient, and *vāra* is already found in *Ṛg Veda*, 2,4,4. The presence of *l* in *bāla*, *vāla* points out to a popular form and the analogy with the non-Aryan words, which we have just now referred to, suggest an Austro-Asiatic origin. The loan can be explained by the importance of wool and hairs in magic and popular religion. It is not at all doubtful

[1] Cf. Bengali *pālak*, the feather or down of a bird. The word has been pointed out to me by Dr. P. C. Bagchi.

that in this respect the Indian thought has been always influenced by the beliefs of the aboriginal populations. One can, for instance, refer to the cult of the hairs of Buddha. In the legend of Rāma, Bālī, the famous monkey-king, the brother of Sugrīva, owed his name to the fact that he was born from the hairs of his mother.

However, the Austro-Asiatic origin of *bāla-* would remain doubtful if this Sanskrit word had not formed the part of a group of which the other elements are certainly non-Aryan. We will see just now, that *kambala śambala* are inseparable from *bāla* and foreign to Indo-Aryan.[1]

The Austro-Asiatic root **bala* was susceptible to have prefixes like *ka*+nasal, in order to form a substantive meaning "a shaggy being." We should not therefore, be astonished to find in Sanskrit a word *kambala*, which means a kind of deer and more precisely, "a sort of deer with a shaggy hairy coat," according to the definition of Monier Williams. As one finds, the description of the animal conforms to the etymology of the name.

From this the use of the word *kambala* for woollen stuff can be easily explained. *Kambala*—in the sense of "woollen stuff"—occurs in the Atharva-Veda (XIV. 2, 66, 67). This word, is doubtless of non-Aryan origin, and has been introduced in the Sanskrit vocabulary prior to the redaction of the Atharva-Veda.

On the other hand the name of "silk-cotton tree" or *Bombax Heptaphyllum* is in Pali *Simbalī* or *Simbala* and in Sanskrit *Śālmalī* or *Śālmala*. One can recognise here

[1] In Tibetan, *bal* means the hair of certain animals, the wool. A composite adjective of this word has been formed *'bal-'bal* which Saratchandra Das translates by "shaggy." It is difficult to decide if these forms are in their origin Tibeto-Burmese, or if *bal* has been borrowed from Indo-Aryan.

the root **bala* which forms a part of the name of cotton or cotton-tree in some Austro-Asiatic languages.

In Pali the root has the prefix *sim*, as in *simbala*, *simbalī*. *Śimbala* already exists in Vedic and means, according to Sāyaṇa "the flower of cotton tree" (*cf.* GELDNER, *Vedische Studien*, 2, 159), that is to say, its bud having the appearance of a big white flower while it is still in its covering.

Skr. *śālmala*, *śālmalī* correspond to Pali *simbala*, *simbalī*, and equally means the *Bombax Heptaphyllum*. These words, however, cannot be the same. *Śalmala* seems to be the Sanskritisation of another form. In the Austro-Asiatic languages, between a root **bala* and a prefix *sa-*, *si-*, one might have intercalated a nasal and a liquid. *Simbala* contains the nasal *m*. *Śālmala* which has got the liquid *l* seems to be the Sanskritisation of **salbala*.

The Sanskrit words *bāla*, *kambala*, *śālmala* form a series in which the idea of hair or wool can be discovered all through. They are differentiated only by the prefixes, *i.e.*, by a process which is foreign to the morphology of Indo-Aryan. It is therefore the Austro-Asiatic root **bala*, which we should suppose to be the origin of all these words.

## II [1]

### SANSKRIT *lāṅgala*, *lāṅgula*, *linga*.

The plough is designated by the following terms in the principal Mon-Khmer and Indonesian languages :

| | |
|---|---|
| Khmer | *aṅkăl* |
| Čam | *laṅan*, *laṅal laṅar* |
| Khasi | *ka-lyṅkor* |
| Tembi | *teṅgāla*. |

[1] Cf. *Memoires de la Socie'te' de Linguistique*, XXII, p. 205 ff.

| | |
|---|---|
| Malay | *teṅgala, taṅgāla* |
| Batak | *tiṅgala* |
| Makassar | *naṅkala.* |

How to explain these different forms? One can suppose either that they have been borrowed from Indo-Aryan (*cf.* Sanskrit *lāṅgalam*), or that they are all derived from an ancient Austro-Asiatic word of which the beginning and the end might have undergone several modifications while the middle part remained more stable.

The first explanation is subject to serious difficulties. The word *lāṅgalam* has no etymology in Indo-Aryan and is certainly not Indo-European. Besides, the counterpart of the words quoted above is found in Annamite, *i.e.*, amongst a people which has never been Indianised like their western neighbours.

In Annamite the word *cày* (pron. *kăi*) is both a verb meaning "to plough" and a noun signifying the "plough." It is possible that in ancient time this word was longer, as we know that in Annamite the tendency towards monosyllabism has been strongly active from early times. Previous to the modern form *kăi*, an ancient one **kăl*, can be supposed. In fact, the final *l*, replaced by *i* in Annamite, is preserved even to-day in several Muong dialects:

| | Annamite | Muong |
|---|---|---|
| "tree" | *kăi* | *köl* |
| "to be hungry" | *doi* | *tol* |
| "two" | *hai* | *hăl* |
| "to fly (of bird)" | *bai* | *pal, pöl* |

Annamite **käl* "the plough," and "to plough" reduced to one syllable, is very similar to the Austro-Asiatic forms, with this difference that they can be separated, and as the Indian influence here is out of question we are brought to suppose that the Mon-Khmer and Indonesian names of the plough have not got an Indo-Aryan origin. *Lāṅgalam* is found already in the Ṛg Veda, but the two *l*-s in the word indicate a vernacular form of it.

The only alternative left to us is to admit that *lāṅgalam* has been borrowed from the non-Aryan peoples of the East since the Vedic times. The same conclusion is inevitable, if one handles a problem of a different kind.

Besides "the plough," the Sanskrit word *lāṅgalam* designates also the "penis." On the other hand, specially in the Sūtras and in the Mahābhārata, a form *lāṅgūla* is found to mean both the "penis" and "the tail" (of an animal). If the equivalence *lāṅgala-lāṅgūla* is authorised, then the semantic evolution of the word would be easily understood. From "penis" one can pass, without difficulty, to the sense of "plough" and "tail." There are evident analogies between copulation and the act of ploughing by which one digs up the earth for depositing the seeds. The problem becomes more complicated from the fact that, almost inevitably, the word *liṅga* which strongly resembles the two other words and has the meaning of "penis" comes in.

Such equivalence is phonetically impossible as long as we are in the Indo-Aryan domain, but they are fully justified in the neighbouring groups. In Čam, for instance, the scolopendra is called *lapan* or *lipan*. In the same language, *kalik* and *kulik*, *kayau* and *kuyàu*, *kabal* and *kubul* are equivalent forms [E. Aymonier and A. Cabaton, *Dictionnaire Čam-français*]. In the Malaya

Peninsula, the tree "pulai" according to Skeat and Blagden is denoted by the following words :

*tingku*
*tengkal*
*tengkol*
*tăngkăl*
*tĕngkul.*

*Tăngkal* is to *tengkul* and *tingku* without final is to *tĕngkul* what *lāṅgala* is to *lāṅgūla* and *liṅga* to *lāṅgala*.

One is thus led to suppose that these multiple and suspicious forms, *liṅga, laṅgala, lāṅgala, laṅgūla, lāṅgūla,* represent diverse aspects of the same word, borrowed by Indo-Aryan from the Austro-Asiatic languages. This hypothesis would be still strengthened if it can be shown that *liṅga* in the sense of "penis" has equivalents in the non-Aryan languages of the East.

Here are the principal names of the sexual organs in the Austro-Asiatic languages :

| | |
|---|---|
| Malay Peninsula | *lak, la, lo.* |
| Stieng | *klau* |
| Bahnar | *k-lao* |
| Khasi | *t-loḥ* |
| Santali | *loc* |
| Ho | *lọc'* |
| Mundari | *lọc'.*[1] |

All these forms appear to be derived from *lak* still found in the Malaya Peninsula. The final *k* is sometimes palatalised into *ḥ* and sometimes disappears completely with the result that the vowel is changed into a diphthong.

[1] Rev. P. O. Bodding writes to me : The word *loc'* is by the Santals considered indecent and is not used before women. There is another word of the same root *lic'*, used about the organ of small boys, but also considered improper.

Here also the hypothesis of a loan from Indo-Aryan is excluded on account of two reasons. The vowel *i* of *liṅga* is never found isolated in any of the Austro-Asiatic words derived from a form in *ă*. Besides the name of "penis" can be found in Annamite with the word *kăk* (Quoc-ngu : *căc*) which doubtless comes from an ancient **k-lak*. We know that the initial consonantal groups were all reduced in Annamite, some before the XVIIth century and the others much later.

On the whole everything tends to show that an ancient Austro-Asiatic root **lak* has given rise to the nominal derivatives ending in *-ala-*, *-ula-*. The existence of a final with vocalism *u* is not solely attested in Indo-Aryan and only by the word *lāṅgūla*. Skr. *laguḍa, lakuṭa*, appear to be copied from *lāṅgūla*, and its meaning of "stick" can be very well derived from "penis." Parallel to Skr. *lāṅgūla* "tail" (of an animal) we find Malay *ekor*, and in the Malay Peninsula, *ikul, ikur, ekor, kur*, with the same meaning.

A certain number of forms which we have examined contain a nasal element which seems to have been inserted in the root. Now we know that in the majority of the Austro-Asiatic languages, the infix *n* seems to form the names of instrument (*cf.* Father. W. Schmidt, *Les peuples Mon-Khmēr*, French translation in B.E.F.E.O., 1907, p. 237ff.). I will quote only one example, similar to the case studied by me : Khmer *čăṅkăut* "helm" derived, by adding an infix from, *čhkăut* "to obstruct, to move against the helm" [E. Aymonier, *Dictionnaire Khmēr-français*, p. xvi]. Hence it is to be noted that amongst the non-Aryan words quoted above, the nasal infix is wanting in those which designate a part of the body : "penis" "tail" (of an animal), while it is found in the names of instrument, for instance in the names of "plough." On the other hand, as to be expected in the case of loan words, Indo-Aryan has no regularity at all in this respect. The contrast *laguḍa-lāṅgūla* has no morphological value at all.

Nasal infix and suffix in *-ūl(a)* seem to co-exist in Khmer. In this language, *bōḥ* signifies "to drive in (a post)" and *bắṅkūl* means the "post." If from Khasi *t-loḥ* "penis" one goes back to the root **lak* from which *lyṅkor* "plough" is derived, one can also go back from *bōḥ* "to drive in" to a root **bak* which explains *bắṅkūl* "post." The first root **lak* is not however entirely hypothetical. One can recognise an alternation of it in Khmer *lŭk* "to drive in (the hand or the finger)" (*Dictionnaire Tandart*). Besides, the Santals have a common word *la* "to dig or make a hole." The derivatives like *lāṅgalam*, etc., express the penetration of plough into female earth. The names of "penis" and of "plough" therefore, signify respectively in the languages in question: "the limb which one drives in" and "the instrument which one drives in."

The insertion of an infix in the body of the root has the effect of lengthening the word, of making it stand wear and tear. The length of the non-Aryan names of plough can be thus explained by reference to other words of the same group derived from the same root. Compare for instance:

Malay: *téṅgala* "plough," *ekur* "tail."
Khasi: *ka-lyṅkor* "plough,"[1] *t-loḥ* "penis."

[1] Indo-Aryan has borrowed even the prefix *kā* of Khasi *ka-lyṅkor*: In the Mahābbārata III. 642, *kalāṅgala* appears to designate a kind of weapon. This way of using the sharp end of plough is not the only instance in the epic. Balarāma is armed with *lāṅgalam* and for this reason, named *lāṅgalin*.

It may seem strange that the Indo-Aryans have borrowed so many words from the Austro-Asiatic languages. Various circumstances have contributed to this result. Some Austro-Asiatic peoples use even to-day, not a plough to furrow but a simple pointed stick for digging holes in which they place the seeds (Skeat and Blagden, *Pagan Races of the Malay Peninsula*, I, p. 348). There the analogy between the penis and the farming instrument is as clear as possible. Profs. Hubert and Mauss point out to me that in Melanesia and Polynesia the farming stick has often the form of a penis. In some Polynesian languages the same word designates the penis and the "digging stick" (*cf.* Tregear, *Maori Comparative Dictionary*, under *ko* and Violette, *Dictionnaire Samoan-français*, under *oga*). It is possible that the aborigines of India, at first, knew the use of this stick and that the name of the instrument for digging the soil has not changed after the introduction of plough.

The persistence of old notions helps us in explaining the legend of the birth of Sītā. In the Rāmāyaṇa I, 66, it is by furrowing the earth with a plough that Janaka gave birth to Sītā. The names are transparent here: Janaka signifies "procreator" and Sītā means a "furrow." The furrow has been personified since the Vedic times. In the Mahābhārata, VII, 105, 3,945, Sītā is a goddess of the harvest. The legend of the birth of Sītā conceals the ancient myth about the production of grain. The same forces are manifested there and the sole action which gives play to them is the penetration of the plough-penis in the female earth.

On the other hand the phallic cults, of which we know the importance in the ancient religions of Indo-China, are generally considered to have been derived from Indian

Saivism. It is more probable that the Aryans have borrowed from the aborigines of India the cult of *liṅga* as well as the name of the idol.[1] These popular practices, despised by the Brahmans were ill-known in old times. If we try to know them better, we will probably be able to see clearly why so many non-Aryan words of the family of *liṅga* have been introduced into the language of the conquerors.

## III

### The Names of Betel.[2]

We know that the betel-leaf, with some other products, is used for the composition of a masticatory much appreciated by the Indian and Indo-Chinese peoples. The following words designate the betel in the Austro-Asiatic languages :

| | |
|---|---|
| Alak | *balu* |
| Khmer | *mluv* |
| Bahnar | *bölöu* |
| Röngao | *bölöu* |
| Sue' | *malua* |
| Lavé | *mělu* |
| Stieng | *mlu* |
| Kha | *blu* |
| Palaung | *plū*. |

[1] While writing this article for a linguistic review I have been led to develop the ideas still further. It is clear from what has been written that the history of a word like *liṅga* is not without importance for the study of religion. I have begun in 1923 a series of study meant to prove that a certain number of myths, legends and tales of Aryan India have been borrowed from the Austro-Asiatic people. The first two of these articles will shortly appear in the publication of the *Ecole Française d'Extrême-orient* (the Jubilee volume) and in the *Journal Asiatique*.

[2] Cf. *Bulletin de la Société de Linguistique*, XXIV, 3, pp. 255-258.

All these forms can be reduced to one type **malū* often having for the initial the alternation *m/b*. The long final is sometimes redoubled into *uv, öu, ua*. The vowel is palatalised into *e, ö* or even reduced to zero.

Siamese has *phlu* with another modification of the initial which remains *labial* but becomes an aspirated surd.

The Annamite dialects have these forms : *trấ'u, giấ'u* which appear to be very different, but the difference is attenuated if we go back to the middle Annamite : in the XVII century Father Alexander de Rhodes still noted *blấ'u* in his dictionary.

The following words are more complicated :

| | |
|---|---|
| Halang | *lamlu* |
| Mon | *ǰablu* |
| Malay Peninsula | *c̆ambai* |
| | *amai* |
| | *ǰ̆ambai* |
| | *ǰ̆ambi*. |

In the first two names the element *mlu/blu* reappears preceded by a prefix : *la-mlu, ǰa-blu*. In the Malaya Peninsula the prefix is *c̆a, c̆am,* or *ǰ̆am* and the ancient root, in which the *l* becomes *i*, is reduced to *mai, bai, bi*.

From that it is possible to explain the Indo-Aryan forms :

| | |
|---|---|
| Sanskrit | *tāmbūlam* |
| Pali | *tambūlī, tambūlaṃ* |
| Prakrit | *tambolaṃ, tamboli*.[1] |

[1] The Persian *tamul* and Arab *al-tambūl* are, no doubt, loans from Indo-Aryan. On the contrary the Chinese transcription *fu-liu* (first mentioned in a work of the third or the beginning of the 4th century) corresponds, as Laufer has well remarked, to the Indo-Chinese forms (*Sino-Iranica*, p. 268, note 2).

We have here a radical *būla/bola* preceded by the affix *tam* or *tām*. The Indo-Aryan element *būla* differs from Austro-Asiatic *balū* only by the permutation of vowels. Moreover, we know that in the Mon-Khmer languages, the prefixes *ka*, *ta* which are used forming the names of animals and plants are often connected with the root through the intermediary of a nasal : *tan*, *tam*, etc. They are doubtless the same affix which, under the forms of *töm* and *döm*, normally precedes the names of trees in Stieng, Bahnar and Cambodian.[1]

The Indo-Aryan *tămbula-*, *ī*, *-am*, which are not known to be Indo-European, is therefore Austro-Asiatic like the creeper itself. This conclusion can be still more strengthened if we go back to the origin of the Indo-Chinese forms.

For preparing the quid of betel, the leaf is rolled up like a cigarette paper. The following words designate in Cambodian the action of rolling up and the connected notions :

| | |
|---|---|
| *mur* | "to roll up" |
| *pomiel* | "to cause to roll up" |
| *mul* | "round" |
| *lomur*, *romul* | "roll." |

We have in Stieng also *mul* "round," *mor* "to roll up (a cigarette)" and Father Schmidt connects these words with : Bahnar *hönul* "zusammenschmieden" (*Grundzüge einer Lautlehre der Mon-Khmer-sprachen*, p. 61).

[1] Many of the Mon-Khmer languages have preserved the ancient prefix even in the name of tree : Nia-hön *tam-loṅ*, Lavé *tom-lōṅ*. Phnong *Tom-chī*, Prou *tom-laṅ*, etc. In consequence of the tendency towards monosyllabism, this ancient prefix has been sometimes (as in Khmer) dissociated from the root and has got an independent existence, playing the role of a numeral of the names of tree and even going so far as to have the force of substantive.

in the domain of the Muṇḍā languages of India which are related to the Austro-Asiatic group, we have in Santali :

*gulu-mulu* "to make round by rubbing between the palms of hands, round, spherical"

*guṛmuṛia* "round, spherical." [1]

In the Austro-Asiatic languages, there is, therefore a verbal root *mul* | *mur* which means "to roll up." The betel leaf, that is to say, the object which one rolls up takes its name probably from this root.

The equivalence of Indo-Aryan and Indo-Chinese forms helps us to explain a Bengali expression, pointed out to me by Dr. S. K. Chatterji. A Hindu caste of Bengal, which has for its main occupation the cultivation and the sale of betel, is called *bārui*<*barai* formed from **bār-* a word which is no longer in use in Bengali, and the suffix *-a-i* which marks appurtenance. The name occurs in a village name *Bārayī-paḍā* in a copper-plate grant of Viśva-rūpa Sena, c. 12th-13th cen. *Bārui*, when Sanskritised, gives *bāru-jīvin* "who lives on **bāru*." There is also the word *baroj* which means the kind of pergola in which the betel vine is grown. *Bār-*, *bar-* evidently designates betel and is clearly related to the Indo-Chinese forms *balu*, etc.

The comparison of words, we have made, is instructive. In the Bengali and the Indo-Chinese forms of the name of betel, the vowel *u* follows the liquid : **bāra*, *balu*, *blu*, etc. On the contrary in Sanskrit and in Pali *u* precedes the liquid, as in the verbal root *mur* | *mul*.

[1] Note that the element *gul-* is found in Indo-Aryan, *cf.* Skr. *gulma*, *gulikā*, etc.

The ancient Indo-Aryan has, therefore, in this respect an advantage over modern languages. Sanskrit and Middle-Indian have preserved the prefix which has disappeared from the modern names of betel and is noted as *tām* in Sanskrit, *tam* in Pali and Prakrit. Therefore, Indo-Aryan *tāmbūla* is probably the most exact transcription of the ancient Austro-Asiatic name of betel.

## IV

### Sanskrit *bāṇa*.[1]

In *Grundzüge einer Lautlehre der Mon-Khmer Sprachen*, pp. 30-31, Father W. Schmidt has compared the following words :

| Mon | Khmer | Bahnar |
|---|---|---|
| " to throw the stones with a bow " { *pɔ̄h* / *pah* | " to throw, shoot to husk (the cotton)" *boḥ* [2] | |
| " this bow " *pnɔ̄h* | " Card for cotton " *phnɔ̄ḥ* | " to draw the bow " { *pŏnah* / *panah* |

A verb *poh*, *pah*, with infixes gives rise to the following derivatives : *panah*, *pŏnah*, *phnɔ̄ḥ* *pnɔ̄h*. The derivation is regular, but it is not *a priori* clear why the same root is used to mean such operations as drawing the bow and husking the cotton. This remarkable fact becomes clear if one observes : 1° that in Stieng *ak* designates an instrument used for preparing the cotton

[1] Cf. *Bulletin de la Société de Linguistique*, XXV, 1, pp. 66-69.

[2] The initial which I transcribe here as *t*, and which Father Schmidt has written *p* is an ancient labial occlusive intermediate between *p* and *b* which M. G. Maspero calls " mixed occlusive." (*Grammaire de la langue Khmère*, p. 65).

before the spinning; and 2° the same word is a name of bow or cross-bow in other Mon-Khmer languages (Danaw *ak*; Riang *ăk* "bow"; Alak *ak* "cross-bow").[1]

On the other hand amongst the Makassar of Celebes, the word *pāna* designates the bow for shooting the arrows and a kind of bow which is also used for washing the cotton (NIEUWENHUIS, *Der Gebrauch von Pfeil und Bogen auf den grossen Sunda-Inseln*, in *Internationales Archiv für Ethnographie*, XIX, pp. 10-11). Sonnerat has observed and sketched a similar instrument in India (*Voyages aux Indes et à la Chine*, Paris 1782, vol. I. p. 108 and pl. 26). "The machine for carding the cotton," says he, "is extremely simple. It is made of a piece of long wood of six to seven feet. To each of its ends is attached a strong string of entrails which, when touched, makes sound like that of the violin (our hatters also have a machine almost similar to it called the *archet* or fiddle-stick). The violin is suspended by a string to that of a bow attached to a plank. The worker holds the violin by the middle in one hand and in the other, with a piece of wood with a pad at the end, stretches quickly the catgut which slips out, strikes the cotton, throws it out, fills it with wind, separates the dust from it and makes it fit for spinning. The elasticity of the bow, which sustains the violin, affords the worker the facility of carrying it from one place to another on the heap of cotton which they come to thrash." The instrument, on the whole, is formed of two bows superposed, because the lower part of the violin which Sonnerat compares

[1] The languages of the Malaya Peninsula have the forms *ig*, *ēg*, *āg* and the equivalent *ĕk* which is preserved in Khmer where it means the bow fixed against the stag-fly (*ĕk khlĕng*). *Cf.* also Santali *ak'*—"bow."

with the *archet* is essentially a vibrating string attached to the ends of a piece of wood. Sir G. Grierson has described a similar but more simple machine in *Bihar Peasant Life*, pp. 64-65.[1]

If the bow for carding the cotton is used in Indo-China as in the Malaya Archipelago and India, it will be shown just now that the words of the same origin similarly designate the shooting, the bow or the arrow, and the cotton.

The tendency of making words monosyllabic has often had the effect of reducing the ancient forms :

| Mon | Khmer | Stieng | Rŏngo | Muong | Annamite |
|---|---|---|---|---|---|
| | | " to draw | the bow " | | |
| *păn* | *băñ* | *păñ* | *păṅ* | *păn* | *băn* |

These words differ from Bahnar *panah*, *ponah*, by the loss of the final and by certain alterations of the nasal. Moreover it is to be noted that the initial of the Khmer form is a ƀ, an unstable *phoneme*, intermediate between the sonant and the surd and of which the equivalent is *b* in Annamite while most of the other languages have *p*.

As regards Mon *pnŏh* "bow for throwing stones" we have :

Čuru : *panan* " bow "
Kon-tu : *paneṅ* " cross-bow "
Sedang : *pöneṅ*, *möneṅ* " cross-bow "
Halang *meneṅ* " cross-bow."

[1] *Cf.* Sanskrit : *tūla-kārmuka, tūlā-cāpa, tūla-dhanus* " cotton-bow, a bow or similarly shaped instrument used for cleaning cotton " Monier-Williams). In the Himalayan dialects we have also : in Lepča, *ki ayok* "to make cotton fine with bow, to card."

In the Kōl or Muṇḍā languages, Santali *banam* means "violin, to play on violin"; the last operation requires the use of an *archet* or a little bow.

On the other hand the Indonesian forms can be reduced in a large number to the type of *panah*. This word designates the bow in Malaya, and in Java, the bow and the arrow Amongst the Dayaks of Borneo, the bow is called *panah*. In numerous languages of the Philippines, *pană* is the name of the arrow, and in Mindanao *panah* is the name of the bow. Lastly in Madagascar *fana, falla*, designate both the bow and the arrow. M. Nieuwenhuis who has studied these Indonesian forms reasonably admits that *panah* must have meant, in ancient times, both the bow and the arrow in all parts of the Malaya archipelago (Art. already referred to, p. 19).

The comparison of the Mon-Khmer forms thus teaches us that *pañah* is derived from the verb *pak, pōh* "to draw the bow" by adding an infix. One understands that the name of instrument, thus formed, designates both the bow and the arrow, *i.e.*, all that is required for drawing the bow. The origin of the Sanskrit word *bāṇa* cannot be, therefore, any longer doubted. It is a loan from the Austro-Asiatic languages and a very ancient loan because the word can be found in the Ṛg-veda, VI, 75, 17. The sonant initial of *bāṇa* was surely not used to translate an Austro-Asiatic *p* in Indo-Aryan. The *b* of the Vedic form is therefore, of a nature to prove the antiquity of b still found in the Cambodian writing of our days.

The Aryans however, certainly knew the use of bow before their entrance into India. Why have they then borrowed from the Austro-Asiatics a word for the arrow?

Probably the arrow made of bamboo was unknown to them and this is why they borrowed the name as well as the instrument itself from the aborigines of India. In fact, in the Malaya Archipelago, the arrow called *nanak* is made of bamboo (*Nieuwenhuis*, pp. 9 and 23). In the same way *bāṇa* designate precisely an arrow of bamboo or of cane in India.

## V[1]

### Sanskrit *karpāsa*.

The verbs *pah*, *pōh*, *ɓōḥ* which have given origin to the name of the bow and the arrow probably do not represent the ancient form of the root. In the Austro-Asiatic languages, a final *h* rises normally from an ancient *s*. In Khmer, for instance, *amɓōḥ* "cotton" has another form *amɓas*. One can suppose, therefore, that the verbs *pah*, *pōh*, *ɓoḥ* had originally a root **ɓas* which meant the action of handling a bow either for throwing projectiles or for carding the cotton.

We now know enough for understanding the formation of the following names which designate cotton in the Austro-Asiatic languages :

Črau *paç*, *baç*

Stieng *pahi*

| | | | |
|---|---|---|---|
| Khmer | *amɓas*, *amɓāḥ* | Rade | *kapas* |
| Bahnar | *kŏpaih* | Malayan, Javanese | *kapas* |
| Sedang | *kŏpè* | Batak | *hapas* |
| Kuoi | *kabas* | Čam | *kapaḥ*. |
| Kŏo | *kopas* | | |

[1] *Bulletin*, XXV, I, pp. 69-71.

At the base of all these forms, whether they have a prefix or not, one finds the root *b̃as*, of which the very unstable initial generally becomes *p* or *b* and the final has been sometimes softened into *h* with a compensatory *i* in some cases. The name of the cotton fibre, therefore, properly means "that which has been husked, carded."

In most of the Austro-Asiatic languages, the prefix is simple : *ka* or *kö*. But we know that in this linguistic family a nasal or a liquid is frequently inserted between the prefix and the root. This can probably explain Khmer : (k)*amb̃as*, (k)*amb̃ŏḥ* of which the initial has disappeared ; and in the same manner we can account for Sanskrit *karpāsa* "the cotton tree" which cannot pal be exined by Indo-European.

Under the form αρπασος the word has entered into the Greek vocabulary and in the book of Esther I, 6. the Hebrew word *karpas* appears to designate like Greek χαρπασος a fine stuff of cotton or flax.

### Sanskrit *paṭa*, *karpaṭa*.

Besides Sanskrit *karpāsa* which comes from an ancient root *b̃as* preceded by the prefix *kar*, it is strange to find in the same language *paṭa* and *karpaṭa* both of which signify "cotton stuff." The existence of *paṭa* and *karpaṭa* side by side permits us to isolate, without hesitation, the prefix *kar*, and points out once again to the Austro-Asiatic domain.

The phonetic and semantic resemblance of *karpāsa* and *karpaṭa* makes us think that these words are exact counterparts. The passage from *s* to *ṭ* is unexpected in Indo-Aryan but in several languages of Indo-China *t* corresponds regularly to *s* of the common family of Mon-Khmer :

| Mon | Khmer | Stieng | Bahnar | Annamite |
|---|---|---|---|---|
| *šok* | *šak* | 'hair' *šok* | *šok* | *tŏk* |

In face of Khmer *bŏs* "to wash, to sweep," we have in Laotien *păt.*

Skr. *karpāsa* on one side and *paṭa*, *karpaṭa* on the other, therefore, must have either been borrowed in successive periods or come from the population speaking the different dialects.

## VI

### Bengali Numeration and Non-Aryan Substratum.

In a series of articles published since 1921 in the *Memoires* and the *Bulletin de la Société de Linguistique de Paris,* I have shown the importance of the Austro-Asiatic languages for the study of Sanskrit and middle Indian languages. By extending the same research to the modern languages of India Prof. S. K. Chatterji has recently indicated that a certain number of substantives in Hindi, Panjabi, Bengali, etc., were borrowed from the Kōl (or Muṇḍā) languages. According to this scholar the Hindi verb *jim-nā* "to eat" would be of the same origin (*The Study of Kōl, Calcutta Review*, 1923, p. 453 ff.) I propose to go a little further and to prove that a Bengali numeral can be explained by the Austro-Asiatic languages.

For "twenty" there are several words in Bengali : the Indo-Aryan forms *bis*, *bis'* and other forms of uncertain origin : *kuri, kuṛi, kuḍi*; the latter ones are found in the Kōl languages.

| | |
|---|---|
| Mahle | *kūri* |
| Birhar | *kūṛi* |
| Juang | *koḍi.* |

The question arises if the Bengali *kuṛi* is a loan from the Austro-Asiatic languages. But a different explanation requires to be discussed at first.

Skr. *koṭi* which signifies "summit" designates the highest number, *i.e.*, 10 millions in ancient Indo-Aryan numeration. It may be asked if it is not the same word, which under the form *kuri,* has taken the meaning of "twenty" in Bengali. This hypothesis is absolutely improbable. One can imagine that a number like twenty conceived at first as the highest number of numeration amongst peoples at a lower state of culture came to be used by their most advanced neighbours for designating a greater number, 100, 1000, etc.; but one can never understand, by what chance a number like 10 millions could be diminished in value and fall down to 20 in a language like Bengali which possesses very large numbers. If *kuṛi* "twenty" and *koṭi* 10,000,000 are, after all, the same word which has successively taken different values, the meaning, "twenty" must be then the most ancient and this is just the case where we can repeat what Codrington said about the number-limit in Melanesian. "A word which, though we may not be able to trace its original meaning, is used at first to signify the highest number and subsequently rises, as the practice of counting advances, to the signification of a higher number than it expressed at first" (*Melanesian Languages*, pp. 248-49). We know that in common Indo-European higher numbers up to 20 existed. If we suppose that *kuṛi* "twenty" is the same as the number-limit *koṭi*, it cannot be therefore Indo-European; and if it be independent of *koṭi* we do not see any other Sanskrit word with which it can be connected. It can be, therefore, suspected to be a loan-word. Its origin now remains to be determined.

What strikes us, at first, is the analogy of the Bengali number *kuṛi* with the same number 20 in some Kōl languages and with the number 10 in the Austro-Asiatic family.

| 20 | | 20 | | 10 | |
|---|---|---|---|---|---|
| Bengali | *kuri* | Mahle | *kūrī* | Palaung | *kŏ* or *se-kūr* |
| " | *kuṛi* | Birhar | *kūṛī* | Biang | *s-kăl* |
| " | *kuḍi* | Juang | *koḍi* | Santali | *gāl* |

Let us go back to the Melanesian facts quoted by Codrington. "In Savo *tale* or *sale* is ten, which in Torres Islands is hundred; the word is no doubt the same. As *tini* may possibly have meant the complete numeration as 'three' in Nengone, and have risen to ten in Fiji, and even to ten thousand in Maori, so *tale* may have signified at first the last number counting when no other number beyond ten was counted and have retained the meaning of ten in Savo while it has been raised as numeration has improved to signify one hundred in Torres Islands" (*ibid*, p. 249).

It may be likewise imagined that in the domain of Austro-Asiatic languages the same word might have signified "ten" and taken later on, under a little different form, the value of "twenty."

The practice of counting by 20 having been preserved in Bengal, the Austro-Asiatic word *kuṛi* might have been retained for meaning "a score" by the side of Indo-Aryan *bis*<*viṃśa(ti)* which signifies "twenty, twice ten."

An exactly parallel fact is observed in Upper Burma; the Siyins, who have the Tibeto-Burman numeration, possess a special word for "score" and it is *kul*:

| | |
|---|---|
| "Ten" | *sôm, hkan, hkat* |
| "Eleven" | *sôm la hkat* |
| "Twelve" | *sôm la ni* |
| "Twenty" | *hkam-ni, sôm-ni, kul* |
| "Twenty-one" | *kul la hkat*[1] |

The name of "score" common to several Kōl languages, Bengali and the language of the Siyins, therefore, goes beyond the Austro-Asiatic domain and encroaches upon the Indo-Aryan and the Tibeto-Burman zones.

The Austro-Asiatic origin of the Bengali number *kuri* can be proved with still more certainty if we can show that this word, besides its numerical value, has a concrete sense in the languages from which it has been borrowed.

Dr. S. K. Chatterji has already indicated (*The Study of Kōl, Calcutta Review*, 1923, p. 455) that the word Kōl is probably an Aryan modification of an old word

[1] Cf. *Gazetteer of Upper Burma and the Shan States*, I, p. 682.

meaning "man." Here are the principal forms of the words signifying "man" and "woman" in the Muṇḍā languages :

| "man" | *haṛ.*<br>*hōrōl* | *har,*<br>*hōrōr* | *haṛa* | *hoṛ* | koro | |
|---|---|---|---|---|---|---|
| "woman" | *kūṛī* | *ērā* | *kūṛī* | *koṛi* | | kol |

Besides these we may compare "son" and "daughter" in Santali :

"son"=*kora hapan.*

"daughter"=*kuri hapan.*

Without insisting on the treatment of the initial, which I shall study elsewhere later on, it can be admitted that a root *kur, kor* is differentiated in the Muṇḍā languages for signifying : man, woman, girl and boy.

That in some cases this root has taken a relatively abstract sense is proved by Santali *koḍa, koṛa,* which signify "one" as in the expression "*koḍa ke koḍa*" "each single one."

Thus one can easily understand that the same root has served the purpose of designating the individual not as an indivisible unity but as a numerical whole. We know besides that amongst a large number of people, said to be primitive, it is the names of the parts of body which are often used for numeration (cf. *Lévy-Brühl, Les fonctions mentales dans les sociétés inférieures,* p. 216). In a recent communication to the French Institute of Anthropology, M Julien has stated that amongst the Malagasis, the word "finger" is added to several numbers from 1 to 5, the number 5 being expressed by a word which originally meant "hand." It can be thus imagined that amongst the Austro-Asiatic peoples also, for expressing 10 or 20, one has thought of "man" provided with 10 fingers if his hands only are considered and with 20 fingers if all the four members [1] of his body are counted.

Thus we can explain the analogy between the root *kur, kor* "man," the number 20 in Muṇḍā *kūṛī, kūṛī, koḍī* and the number 10 in the Austro-Asiatic family *kö, se-kūr, skall, gäl.*

Similar facts can be observed in other parts of the Austro-Asiatic world. In Annamite *moi* which signifies "each, all," like Santali *koḍa,* means also "the savage"; this word is hardly different from *muoi* which is the number 10. In Khasi there is *u briw* "man" and *shi phew* "ten." The consonantal group *br* has been here contracted into *ph* as it generally happens in the monosyllabic languages. It seems, therefore, that in Annamite and in Khasi the word "man" and the number "ten" are two forms of the same root.

The identity of the number 20 and the name of man, can be also observed in Mandingue, one of the most important languages of Western Africa. "In this language," as Professor Delafosse writes to me, "the number 20, when it is not multiplied, is called *muγa* (*moughan*), a word which can be connected with *moγo̮* or *mopo̮* (*mòghò* or *mòrhò*) signifying "man" in the sense of human being, without any consideration of sex. When the number "twenty" is multiplied, *muγā* is no longer used but *moγo̮* or *mopa̮*; thus "sixty" is called *moγo̮ saba,*

Broke tells us how a Dayak of Borneo, before counting up to 45, used the fingers of his hands, and then those of his feet, and when he had exhausted the fingers of his f he came back to the fingers of hands. (*Ten Years in Sarawak*, I, pp. 139-40.)

(literally "man three," three men) and sixty men, *moyo moyo saba*, exactly "three men of men." Lastly, for the number "forty" the word *debe* is often used; it properly signifies a mat for bedding: the natives of the country say that the reason of this is that the mat evokes a couple of human beings (man and woman) who lie down together on it; a man, with his 20 fingers, represents "twenty"; a mat on which two men lie down, represent "two twenties."

The habit of using the word "man" for designating the numbers 10 and 20 is not, therefore special to Muṇḍā languages, not even to the Austro-Asiatic family only. The fact that in Muṇḍā *gäl* "10" differs much more than *kūrī* "20" of the root *kur*, *kor* "man," indicates quite clearly that these words have not certainly the same history. Besides the need of distinguishing 10 and 20 for avoiding confusion, other circumstances might explain the deviation observed between *gäl* and *kūrī*. In Cambodia one counts still by 5, saying 5·1, 5·2, for 6 and 7, etc. In most of the Austro-Asiatic languages one still counts by ten but I do not know any language of this family in which one counts by scores, outside the domain of Muṇḍā. It seems, therefore, that the system of numeration has been transformed by innovations which, no doubt, go back to different periods and probably radiate each from a certain family. The analogy of Riang *s-kal* and of Santali *gäl*[1] seems to indicate that one should

[1] Conrady has tried to establish a relation between the transformation of initial sonants into surds and the phenomenon of contraction of a prefix with the root in Tibetan. His theory should not be accepted without reserve (cf. *Les Langues du Monde*, p. 364). It is possible that we may have here a fact of the same order but in an inverse sense.

search in the Mon-Khmer languages for the origin of the computation by ten, while *kūrī* "20," very similar to the name of man in Muṇḍā or Kōl languages would be an innovation properly Kōl. Unfortunately we still ignore too many things for being able to determine the history of language as well as that of civilisation with certitude in this case.

# PART II

# SANSKRIT AND DRAVIDIAN

BY

JULES BLOCH

# Sanskrit and Dravidian[1]

A good illustration of the influence of substratum in the evolution of languages may be found in certain transformations undergone by the Indo-European language in India. A category of consonants—the cerebrals in Sanskrit—corresponds, in a striking manner, with some consonants in the phonetic system of the two other families of language. Now to which of the two Non-Aryan families must one attribute this innovation in the Aryan language? Of the two Non-Aryan families one, the Munda, is the language of a people scarcely civilised who now forms barely a hundredth part of the entire population of India. The other, the Dravidian, is spoken by about one-fifth of the entire population. The South-Dravidian again is the vehicle of an old civilisation. Another member of the same family, the Brahui now existing isolated far to the west in the heart of Beluchistan, is an evidence of the ancient area of expansion of Dravidian before the Indo-European invasion, at least to one who knows how to interpret geographical indications. In the absence of direct historical evidence these considerations have generally led one to think that Dravidian is the language which has been replaced by Indo-European and that the peculiarities of this language explain the innovations in Indo-Aryan. The two points on which

[1] *Bulletin de la Société de Linguistique de Paris*, XXV, I, p. 1 *seq.*

we would like to make some observations are these : the value of the proofs brought forward in support of this thesis (and summarised as far as phonetics and grammar are concerned by Prof. Sten Konow in the *Linguistic Survey of India,* Vol. IV, p. 278 *seq.*. to which we refer here once for all) and the sources of information available on this point.

Before we discuss the value of the alleged evidences we would like to point out certain difficulties of a general character. In the first place the geographical isolation of Brahui is susceptible of several interpretations. It is certainly not impossible that the Brahuis for long centuries might have inhabited the place where we find them now and from the same barren plateau might have watched the migrations and historical incidents in their neighbourhood without being affected by them. But in a country like India which has been incessantly disturbed by migrations it is equally possible that they have come to their present locality in a comparatively recent epoch (*cf.* Denys Bray, *Census of India,* 1911, Vol. IV, Beluchistan, p. 168 *seq.*) as a result of the movements of the same kind and perhaps due to the same causes which have brought the Oraons and the Malers of Dekhan to Chota-Nagpur or the nomad tribes of Dekhan studied by Prof. Sten Konow in Vol. XI of the *Linguistic Survey* to all over Northern India (the first of the two groups speaks the Dravidian language and Prof. Sten Konow is inclined to attribute a Dravidian origin to the second also (*J. As.,* 1923, I, p. 136). The Brahuis of to-day are not absolutely sedentary ; they go out of their country for temporary emigrations and for forays and even for true emigrations (D. Bray, *ibid,* p. 45 *seq.*). Some peculiarities of their language would also seem to show that they have come from elsewhere :

specially by the substitution of initial *b*—for *v* in Dravidian Brahui is connected with Canara, Kurukh, and Malto (the last two are spoken by the Oraon and the Maler mentioned above) but it is different from the contiguous Iranian (Afghan, Beluchi) and the Indo-Aryan (Punjabi, Sindhi) languages. Similarly the absence of cerebral nasal in Brahui connects it with the oriental dialects, either Indo-Aryan or Munda (*J. As.*, 1911, I, p. 165).

Even if in our imagination we fill up the entire gap between Beluchistan and the Dekhan the natural links would be the coastal regions of the lower Indus and Gujrat; in fact certain invasions have actually followed the same path. The plains of the Punjab and the valley of Ganges which are pre-eminently the lands of Sanskrit will however remain outside the continuous zone thus reconstructed, and nothing stands in the way of supporting that this territory has been occupied by non-Dravidian languages before the Indo-European invasion. The consideration of the phonetic substratum seems to support this hypothesis. The regions in question ignore the use of cerebral *ḷ* which is current in the rest of India from the lower Indus to Ceylon (Jules Bloch, *Langue Marathe*, p. 147). Some languages belonging to a family, now unknown, might have been actually in use in this region in ancient times. But even without appealing to the unknown we know that the Munda dialects in which *ḷ* is wanting are to-day disseminated over the table-lands on the northern border of the Dekhan. Might they not have been driven back there by the Indo-European? Prof. Przyluski has already given some examples of the contribution to the Sanskrit vocabulary made by the dialects of the Austro-Asiatic family to which Munda is connected.[1] (MSL, XXII, p. 202 *seq.*, BSL, XXII, p. 118, p. 255 *seq.*) This proves either the substitution of one language by the other or their mutual contact in ancient times. The geographical evidence is therefore ambiguous.

On the other hand certain necessary precautions have not been taken in utilising properly the linguistic data. The Dravidian language which has almost always been chosen for comparison is Tamil, which in fact is the best known of all the dialects for various reasons. Even if we admit that from the Vedic up to the present time Tamil has changed very little there still remains the fact that the domain of this Dravidian dialect is the furthest off from the region of Vedic civilisation. On this principle alone, it should have been the last one to be taken into consideration for the sake of comparative study. As Mr. E. Tuttle has very well said (*American Journal of Phil.*, XL, p. 76) : "If we want to understand the history of the languages of the South we should begin from the Northern side." In fact, our knowledge of the Dravidian languages of the north is very imperfect and certainly has been very recently acquired, so much so that when it is possible to recognise the interchange of vocabulary between Dravidian and Indo-Aryan it is very difficult to determine which is the lender and which is the borrower though it is absolutely necessary to know the

[1] When this was in the press an important article by Prof. Sylvain Lévi has appeared in *J. As.*, July-Sept., 1923, in which he has shown that a certain number of ethnic names of ancient India can be explained by the morphological system of the Austro-Asiatic languages. Lack of sufficient fixity of Sanskrit forms seems to be the result of diverse efforts to transcribe names still in use and as such is an evidence of the late survival of those languages.

common form of Dravidian ~~(in a general way)~~. We know it very little and we search for it still less. In fact Tamil represents very badly the common Dravidian language. Evidence in support of this statement will be found below. With these general reservations, however, what is the value of the alleged proofs about the influence of Dravidian on Indo-Aryan.

It is through phonetic innovations that the influence of a linguistic substratum is most clearly visible. Thus the consonant mutation of Armenian can be directly explained by a comparison with southern Caucasian (Meillet, *Esquisse.. de l'arm. class.*, p. xiv; *Caract. des lang. German*, p. 40, MSL. XIX, p. 164, *Introd.* [5], p. 11). Similarly in India, the co-existence of cerebral consonants next to dentals in Indo-Aryan, in Dravidian and also in Afghan, an Iranian language contiguous to Indo-Aryan and to Brahui, cannot be easily considered as a mere chance.

But the Armenian and Indian cases cannot be exactly compared with each other. In Sanskrit there is no change in the articulation of an entire series of sounds. The cerebral series has not come out of the total transformation of the dental series but has come into existence along with it under determined circumstances through several stages of evolution. As regards the most ancient period, the first question is that of the adaptation of the two Aryan series to the two indigenous ones. For in India the dental series properly so-called had added to it the series which rests on the existence of an ancient Indo-Iranian *š* (*sh*-sound); to this (*sh*-sound) were added consonants which accommodated themselves to it; moreover *r* replaced the sonant *sh*-sound (*ž*) and through accommodation brought new consonants into existence in the same series: the whole of this series was pronounced as cerebrals.

Later on, the occlusives ṭ and ḍ, the nasal ṇ and ḷ have replaced the ancient intervocalic dentals under different historical and geographical circumstances (*cf. Langue Marathe,* pp. 95, 125, 137, 147); the withdrawal of the point of articulation in these cases is the sign of the weakness of the consonant. Finally the initial dental occlusive has been, but rarely, cerebralised (*ibid*, p. 124).

Such is 'in general' the history of the cerebrals in Indo-Aryan. In the greatest part it is sufficient in itself and Dravidian does not throw any light on it. On the contrary it contradicts it in certain cases.

Let us pass on to the fact that cerebral ḷ form, which represents normally in Vedic intervocalic ḍ, disappears from classical Sanskrit, while it is still in current use in Dravidian. It was simply an archaism according to M. Meillet (*IF*, XXXI, p. 123): an archaism which was perhaps necessary in the Ganges basin where ḷ was lacking, as was seen above. But here are some of the more characteristic facts.

The extension of initial cerebral occlusives which is the most obscure event in the history of the Indo-Aryan consonants, suggests at the very first instance explanation by the substratum: but Dravidian does not allow the use of the cerebral initials. On the contrary, Dravidian allows final cerebral nasals and liquids, which are unknown in Sanskrit.

There is, therefore, nothing to justify the assertion that Indo-Aryan cerebrals are of indigenous origin. The local pronunciation has rendered the development of this class possible; and in this sense the action of the substratum is undeniable. But it is necessary at once to insist upon the fact that the Munda languages have dentals and cerebrals just like Dravidian, and nothing, therefore, stands in the way of attributing theoretically the origin of the Sanskrit pronunciation to the action of a substratum of either Munda or some other language connected with it, if not of a fourth linguistic family still unknown.

Another fact alleged is the progressive extension of *l* in classical Sanskrit at the expense of *r*, used almost exclusively by Vedic in accord with Iranian. But it is known that *l* in Sanskrit is not really an innovation; it marks on the contrary the cropping out in literature of the dialects more conservative on this point than the most ancient Vedic and Iranian (Meillet, *IF*, XXXI, p. 124; *Bhandarkar Memorial*, p. 357); it is Iranian and Vedic which form the exception and for which the question of the substratum must be put. Here, too, Munda possesses *l* just as Dravidian.

It will be seen later on that the Dravidian languages have, in the course of their history, eliminated consonant groups either by accommodation or by insertion of vocalic elements; on the other hand this is known to be just the characteristic of Middle-Indian. But in the Aryan group the evolution in question, although it was to reach its full development only in middle-Indian, is not only anterior to the Vedic period but goes farther back; without referring to the law of Bartholomae, one can attribute to it at least the origin of Skr. *cch*. Besides, if the tablets of Kikkuli of Mitani (Jensen, *Sitzb.*, *Berlin*, 1919, p. 368 and in the last place Forrer, *ZDMG*[2], I, 2, p. 252 ff.) really show the existence of a dialect belonging to tribes akin to those who brought Sanskrit to India, as the suffix of *Aika* "one" seems to indicate, proof will be found in *tēra* "three," *satta* "seven" of this old "Middle-Indian" that the tendency in question had arisen long before the contact of Aryan with Dravidian: unless, adding a new hypothesis to others, we want to make Dravidian come from the same region as that of Aryan and almost at the same time. The hypothesis is not absurd; the origin of Dravidian has already been looked for in this direction; but it has not sufficient ground to serve as an explanation.

On the contrary, the unification of the sibilants which equally characterises classical Middle-Indian is very recent; even to-day it has not been carried out either in the languages of the mountainous regions of the North-West nor in Gypsy. It seems to be due to the action of the substratum (*cf.* Michelson, *JAOS*, XXXIII, p. 146); but this substratum cannot be located in the North-West since in this region we find first of all Vedic, then the dialects of the inscriptions of Aśoka and last of all, the modern languages—all of which distinguish at least sibilants and *sh*-sounds. It can be Munda as well as Dravidian as the documents of the *Linguistic Survey* show that Munda like Dravidian has only one series of sibilants.

Dravidian, as we know it, admits spirants like Iranian; Indo-Aryan has not any and according to M. Meillet (*IF*, XXX, p. 120) that is the pre-eminent characteristic of Indo-Aryan as distinguished from Iranian: if this preservation is to be explained by local circumstances, then amongst the known languages, Munda only must be referred to, since, unlike Dravidian (and like Aryan), it has aspirate occlusives and lacks spirants.

A curious fact that might be noted here is the continuous character of the Sanskrit sentences, which has given rise to the rules of *sandhi*, because Tamil and Canarese admit a rigorous *sandhi* in writing. But the same languages in their spoken form ignore it; Gondi and Kurukh also ignore it. In so far as these literary languages admit this *sandhi*, it is certainly due to the influence of Sanskrit; and even in Sanskrit it is probable that the use of the rules in question has very much surpassed in extension the real use; Aśoka ignores them absolutely.

There is, therefore, no clear phonetic proof of the action of Dravidian on Indo-European, at any rate, in ancient times. Some agreements can be discovered at present, on the frontiers of the two domains. Thus the diphthongisation of initial (*y*)*e*—and (*w*)*o* in Marathi and Telugu (*Langue Marathe*, p. 33; Prof. Turner also, has pointed out, *Ind. Antiq.*, 1921, p. 99, the same phenomenon in Nepali) or the alternation *č* : *ċ* according to the nature of the following vowel in Marathi and Telugu; a Munda language of the same region still affords an alternation of *č* and *ċ* in a similar way. There is a great difference between facts like these, recent and quite local, and the supposed influence of one language family on another at the time when the Aryans entered India.

Phonology therefore cannot throw any clear light on it, morphology will necessarily throw even less because at the time of the substitution of languages the grammatical system borrows much more thoroughly than the phonetic system. Inspite of all this, are there in Indo-Aryan some exceptional facts revealing certain grammatical uses which might have survived the ruin of the entire system?

The reduction of the verbal system of the Vedas and the inverse extension of nominal phrases have been explained as the action of Dravidian. But it must be noticed that the Dravidian system is the same for all tenses and that in Sanskrit, the past tenses only have disappeared. As far as the perfect is concerned it may be remarked with all precision that Dravidian ignores reduplication and the reduplication in Munda has only intensive and conative values (*Ling. Surv.*, IV, p. 46); on the contrary, the existence of tense suffixes in these two families (*ibid*, pp. 49, 172, etc.) would have been rather a support at least for the Aorist stems. In fact the process by which all these forms have been replaced by nominal ones is found also in Iran. There is therefore, no occasion to insist unreasonably on the very outward resemblance of the two isolated forms of masculine nominative singular, Skr. *kṛtavān* "who has done, he has made," from a stem—*ta-vant*, known in Iranian (Brugmann, *Grundriss*, II, 1, p. 463) and in Tamil *sey-d-avan*, which is formed on a very different principle and moreover has not the same use: it is in fact *sey-d-ān* which has the function of a verb; the relation is the same in Kurukh between *is'us* "the breaker" and *es'as* "he has broken," where the alternation of the stem emphasizes the difference of value.

The reduction of genders of the substantive which characterises modern Indo-Aryan, does not admit any further local explanation, although it is posterior to Sanskrit. The question therein is of a tendency common to all Indo-European which is however far from ending in such a rapid and downright manner as Armenian and Persian where the disappearance of gender is due to the substratum (Meillet, *Esquisse...de l'arm, class.*, p. xiv; a statement which is to be a little modified as far as the Armenian is concerned, *R. des Ét. Armén*, 1923, pp. 3-4). In India gender disappears completely from the eastern languages only, and in fact there and there only the question is undoubtedly of the action of a Tibeto-Burman substratum. Though on some points the distinction between the animate and the inanimate exists in some isolated cases, the question is of a human fact of which the equivalents can be easily found outside India; finally, the classification of Dravidian nouns into *mahat* "great" and *amahat* "small" (the first category includes gods, demons and men; the second, animals and things) differs from the Munda classification into animate and inanimate (whatever has been said on all this in *Langue Marathe*, p. 199, should be corrected).

If Dravidian cannot explain the alterations of the Indo-European system can it inversely account for the abnormal preservation? Indo-Aryan is the only one of the Indo-European languages which has retained the relative pronoun. But Dravidian ignores the relative; Munda also equally ignores it.

The only thing left is to consider some general facts of recent date in the two families due to a fundamentally analogons structure. Dravidian in fact operates only by the addition of suffixes, differently from Munda which uses prefixes and infixes. To illustrate the course of a parallel evolution nothing more is necessary than to mention that the determinative elements of noun come after an oblique case in the two families (Munda has also postpositions which are suspected of being partly borrowed from modern Indo-Aryan, *Ling. Surv.*, IV, pp. 41, 85.) The resemblance of Tam. Tel. *ku* "to," Can. *ke*, Kur. *ge*, with Hindi *ko*, *ke*, etc., is accidental unless it is admitted, on the contrary, to be a borrowing by Dravidian from Indo-Aryan. Even an isolated expression, like the use of a word signifying "having said" in Indo-Aryan, to mark the subordination of propositions, is not to be invoked here; because it is not only in use in Marathi and Singhalese, languages in contact with Dravidian, but also in Nepalese and Bengali and at least in one language of the Tibeto-Burman group, the Boḍo (*Langue Marathe*, p. 272 and Errata).

One is, therefore, ultimately led to search for the Dravidian elements of Sanskrit only in the vocabulary. But the history of vocabulary is absolutely different from phonetic or grammatical evolution, and the loan of words is essentially different from the facts of a substratum. The facts of a substratum result from the unconscious blending of two systems existing amongst the same people; the loan results from a willing effort to add elements taken from outside to the mass of the vocabulary. The loan proves the contact of the two languages and not the substitution of the one by the other. On the other hand it is often difficult to recognise in what sense the borrowing is made between two given languages and to make sure that it has not been made by each of the two languages from a third one, known or unknown.

Lastly, where it becomes clear that Aryan is the borrower, it is necessary to determine from what group of Dravidian the loan has been taken and also to draw from it information for the history of Dravidian itself. There is no question of undertaking that work here, which is still impossible, but we only want to point out by some examples, the interest and the present aspect of the question.

The Vedic (and Indo-European) name for horse, *açva*, is no longer represented to-day in Indo-Aryan except on the confines of the Iranian world where the corresponding word is still living (Grierson, *Piśāca Language*, p. 73, and the list of *Ling. Survey*, No. 68). The word which has replaced it in all other parts of the country occurs in the Srauta Sūtra of Āpastamba—a text which appears to be of southern origin (*cf.* Bühler, *SBE*, II, p. xxx) under the form *ghoṭa*. Mr. J. Charpentier has tried (*KZ*, XL, p. 441) to identify this word with German *gaul*; this eqvivalence would be strange by itself; Prof. Sommer has shown (*IF*, XXXI, p. 362) that this Germanic word has its correspondents in Slavonic and not in Indian. On the other hand, the similarity of *ghoṭa* with some Dravidian forms with the same meaning has long been recognised: Tel. *gurramu.*; Can. *kudure*; Tam. *Kudirei* (Gondi *Kōṛā* is suspected to be borrowed from Hindi *ghoṛā* like Kui *gōḍā*); the Dravidian form which has preceded the Hindi word amongst the Gonds is undoubtedly that which accounts for Gadaba *Kruṭā* and Savara *kurtā*, alone of their kind in Munda. The Brahui *hulli* is out of the question; on the value of initial *h*, *cf.* on one hand Br. *hal* "rat," *hēṭ* "goat," *hīn* "to deposit" and Tam. *eli*, *āḍu*, *īn*; on the other Br. *hur* and Gondi *hūṛk*, *kui sūḍ* (*cf.* Tuttle, *Am. J. Phil.*, XL, p. 84).

It is easy to reconstitute the common prototype of all these forms. **ghutr—*. In the same process one gets some important data for the history of Dravidian phonetics:

1st. The consonantal group has been eliminated in Telugu by total assimilation, in Tamil and Canarese by vocalic insertion.

2nd. In the last two languages, the intervocalic surd is changed into a sonant. In Tamil, at any rate, the date of this alteration is rather late, *cf.* MSL, XIX, p. 89; for Canarese an indication is to be found in the fact that the name of Maski, the village where an inscription of Aśoka has been discovered is still *Piriya-masangi* in a Calukya inscription (H. Krishna Shastri, *The Maski Rock Edict*, p. 1).

3rd. In the same languages the initial consonant is changed into a surd. Here from the Dravidian standpoint the rule is not clear : there are two series of corresponding forms. In fact M. Subbaya in his articles in the *Indian Antiquary*, 1909 (where he always attributes wrongly the surd to common Dravidian) has given a series of equivalent forms : Tam. *k*—Can. Tel. *g*—(pp. 205, 217 ; *cf.* for the dental p. 200). But in his Dictionary of Canarese, Kittel gives a good number of examples of the Tam. Can. *k*, Tel. *g* similar to that in the name of horse : thus Tam. Can. *kādal* "love," Tel. *gādilu* ; Tam. Can. *kīṛu* "to scratch," Tel. *gīru* ; Tam. Can. *kuṟi* "sheep," Tel. "*gorre*" ; Tam. Can. *Kuḷi* "hole," Tel. "*goyyi*." The interpretation of the facts is difficult ; but the antiquity of the sonants in Dravidian remains undisputable.

If it were certain that the Sanskrit word was borrowed from Dravidian, one could have rightly deduced at once a fourth observation, more important than all the previous ones. In that case the most ancient Dravidian, in fact, would have had aspirate consonants, either a dialect in contact with Indo-Aryan having developed aspirates in some cases or the aspirates having belonged to common Dravidian. There is nothing inadmissible in this view ; the interval is extremely long between the epoch when *ghoṭa* was admitted into Sanskrit and the late date—very likely the 5th century A.D.—when the alphahets of the North were borrowed by the principal Dravidian languages : in fact it is known that the characters which mark the aspirates in Indo-Aryan are wanting in these alphabets. But in this case it must be asked if Dravidian itself is not a language brought to the Dekhan, its present area: because the loss of aspiration is one of these typical facts which immediately makes one think of the action of the substratum: this substratum could not have been Munda which possesses aspirates. Dravidian, the language of the Dekhan, therefore, would have been at first a language of the North and the horse, in fact, is in India really an animal of the North: it has been discovered in a fossil state in the Siwalik mountains; and the Vedas specially mention the horses of Sind and the Sarasvati (*cf.* Crooke, *Things Indian*, p. 253 ff.; Macdonell-Keith, *Vedic Index*, under *açva*). Thus one would again fall back on a hypothesis, similar to the one already mentioned, about the contact of two languages in the pre-historic period in anterior Asia; but it will have this time another degree of historical probability; the history of ancient India can be explained to a great extent by the successive floods of invasions of which the first is only an anticipated consequence of the second: the Dravidians might have preceded the Aryans, as the Śakas preceded the Kuṣaṇas and as later on the Kuṣaṇas again preceded the Huns. The difference would be this that the Dravidians and Aryans imposed their languages on India.

Thus questions that are brought forward are important at least in the hypothesis that *ghoṭa* was taken from Dravidian. But the name of the horse is essentially a name subject to renewal and no one can foresee whence the new name would be taken. One may think of *ross*, *pferd* and *gaul* without speaking of *mähre* and of *stute* and, in another domain, of *caballus* and *mannus.* If Dravidian be the borrower, or if both languages took the same word, perhaps along with the specimens of a particular breed, for instance, of Iran or of Arabia[1] the entire edifice, phonetic as well as historical, will collapse.

The name of the "ass" suggests a problem analogous to that of the "horse." The identity of R. V. *gardabha* (on the suffix Skr. *-bha*—Gr. -φο, etc., of the names of animals, see Brugmann, *Grundriss*, II, 1, p. 389), Hindi *gādhā* etc. (borrowed freely in Dravidian, in Munda and in Assam by the Khasi; see the lists of *Ling. Survey*, 74) on the one hand, and Tel. *gāḍide*, Can. *kalte, katte*, Tam. *kaludei* on the other hand is evident (Kurukh *gadṛārnā* "to bray." Is it Dravidian or Aryan? In the Celebes the language of the Bug tribes has a form borrowed from the Dravidian, *kaledde*); a prototype **gard* accounts for all the forms if only because the rule concerning the consonantal groups previously stated admits of an alteration in the case of a liquid preceding the occlusive instead of following it. In fact one finds the use of the Can. *kalte, katte*, in the word for "rice," Can. *akki*, Tam. *ariçi*, forms of which the comparison is sufficient to suggest an ancient **arki*, or in the word for the "cat" (admitted in Sanskrit at the time of the epic, Skr. *biḍ-āla-*, *bil-āla-*, *bir-āla-*, Kāçm *brar*, Syrian Gypsy *blari*, Hindi *bilāri*, *bilayā*, *billī*, etc., from which secondarily Can. etc. *pilli*; see the lists of the *Ling.*

[1] M. Autran would like to explain the Egyptian word *ḥtr* which means the carriage and the horse as a loan from an unknown language of Southern Arabia. We know that horse appeared in Egypt only towards the 16th cen. B.C.

*Survey*, No. 71), Can. *berku*, *bekku*, Kur. *berxā*, Gondi *bǎkǩ* Tam. *verugu*.[1]

What is the origin of this **gard* common to Indo-Aryan and Dravidian ? The presence of this word in *Ṛgveda* has led etymologists to search for an Indo-European origin. Some connect it with the Romance word for "mule" admitted very late into Latin (*v.* Walde, under *burdo* ; *cf. Ernout, Elém. dial. du vocab. latin*, p. 132) ; Prof. Wackernagel has thought of English *colt*, which primarily designates the little ones of an animal, and particularly in the Bible and in Middle English the young one of a camel or an ass ; agreements which are very poor and far-fetched—the ass has no Indo-European name. The ass is an animal of Asia ; it is rare in India except in the Western regions (*cf.* Lévi, *BEFEO*, IV, p. 568). The Mediterranean name of ass, Gr. ὄνος etc., appears to come from Western Asia ; *khara*—, which is wanting in the most ancient Sanskrit texts, is known only in India and in Iran ; hence it is not at all astonishing that the Vedic words *gardabha* —and *rāsabha*—have not any corresponding Indo-European terms, just as it is natural that Brahui has a name, which as far as we know, belongs only to it, (*bǐs*). The probabilities are, therefore, in favour of **gard*

[1] Tamil has another word *pūnei*, *pūçei* ; one is inclined to connect *pūçu*, Can. *pūsu*, and Tel. *pūyu*, "to smear" with one another : the Semantic relation will recall classical Skr. *mārjāra* (which has the same suffix as *bir-āla*) ; but we find in Munda *pūsī*, in Tibetan *piši* (beside *byila* borrowed from Indo-Aryan. *cf.* Laufer, *Tibetan Loan Words* in. 64), in Afghan *pišo*, in Persian *pušek* ; in the North-West of India *puši*, and *būši* (Grierson, *Piš. Lang.*, p. 66) in Brahui *piši*. The words are independent of each other and are results of onomatopoeia ; the same is found in Europe, *puss*, etc.

being a local word existing on the confines of India and Iran. Hence we are again faced by the fundamental problem: has Dravidian supplied the word to Aryan and is it the first language that the Aryans met with in India? Or have both Dravidian and Sanskrit borrowed the name of the ass from a third language which, at any rate (to judge by the lists of the *Linguistic Survey*), can be neither Munda nor a language related to the mysterious *Burušaski*? Or lastly is it not Dravidian which took the word from Sanskrit? It is impossible to give an answer for the time being.

That the two families have been in contact with each other for long, there is no room for doubting. There are facts which prove it but which raise new problems too.

One has identified (G. A. Jacob, *J.R.A.S.* 1911, p. 510; D. R. Bhandarkar, *Anc. Hist. of India*, p. 26) *maṭacī* found in the Chāndogya-Upaniṣad with Can. *midice* "grass-hopper" The relation between Skr. *ma-* and Can. *mi-* is not without analogy; it is, for instance, difficult to separate the different words for "black pepper," Skr. *marica*, Tam. *milagu*, Can. *meṟasu* from each other. But one is led to ask if a family of Dravidian words expressing size is not entirely borrowed from Aryan, Skr. *mahā*, Can. *mige*, Tam. *migei* "abundance," Tam. Can. Tel. *mincu* *minju* "greatness, excellence," Can. *mikku* "excess," etc. (*cf.* Caldwell, *Compar. Gramm.*[3], p. 602); Kur. *mechā* "high," *megrō* "elder." If it be so, then of the two languages Aryan may be considered as having the most prestige and very likely as being the least open to borrowing and all the more to the phonetic and morphological influence of a Dravidian substratum.

There are cases in which a language would submit to the influence of another without borrowing complete words. It can be asked whether the word for "wheat" which is found from the Yajurveda onwards, *e.g.*, *godhūmāh* (in the singular in the Śatapatha Brāhmaṇa) does not owe its form to such an influence. This word apparently significative but having an absurd signification ("smoke of the cow"), cannot be separated from the Iranian *gandum*, which being in no way significative, is necessarily the most ancient. Cannot the deformation undergone by the word in India be explained by the presence of a word with the same meaning in Dravidian, Can. *gōdi*, Tam. *kōdi*, Toda *kodj*? One would be inclined to explain, by an inverse contamination, the double aspect in classical Sanskrit of the word for "fan"—*vījana* and *vyajana*—alternating in an abnormal way; it looks as if that a word expressing the instrument derived from the root of Can. *bīsu*, Tam. *viçu*. Tel. *vīcu*, *vīsaru*, and *vivu* "to swing, to fan, to blow" was at the time of its introduction into Sanskrit, formed on the model now of *vij*. and now of *vy-aj-*.

These diverse aspects, presented by the problem of loans are not the only ones. There are others in which non-Munda languages must be counted.

Let us at first come back to the names of animals. A name which has a good chance of being Indian is that of the "peacock" and it would be in no way astonishing if in face of Rv. *mayūra* and in the forms supplied by Aśoka, *mora*—at Girnar, *majura*—in the North-West, *majūla* at Kalsi and Jaugada, we find a group of Dravidian forms: Tam. *mayil*, Can. *maylu* and *navil*, Tel. *mali* Gondi *mal*. The identity of the names is evident; but it is difficult to determine the ancient form. If it is admitted with Mr. T. Michelson (*J.A.O.S.*, XXX, p. 84, n. 6) that the *-j*, of the inscriptions of the North-West is "Magadhism" one still remains embarrassed by the co-existence of the forms with *-l-* and *-r-*. Should one say that the contact took place between Dravidian and the Eastern dialects of Sanskrit? It would be a further definition of great value. But Eastern Munda possesses a word of similar appearance, with *r*; *e.g.* Savara, *mära*, Santali *marak'*; and this word re-appears in Indo-China: Mōn *mrak*, Bahnar *mra* (to tell the truth, Father Schmidt connects these two forms with Skr. Pali *barhī*, derived from *barha*—another word of unknown origin). One does not know if the two series should be put together or not.

Is the Tamil word *palam* "ripe fruit" copied from or the original of the Vedic *phála*—? Here the difficulty is manifold. One can imagine the Indo-European etymologies (*cf.* Uhlenbeck, s.v.; Wackernagel *Altind. gr.*, I, pp. 120, 123; M. Meillet proposes Old Slav. *plodŭ* "fruit"). But one can also refer to Can. *paṇ*, Tel. *poṇḍu* Kur. *panjqā* "fruit," possibly even to Brahui *pirs* "to swell up:" the nasal does not cause any absolute difficulty, Canarese has *menasu* by the side of *melasu* quoted above as the designation of "pepper"; it gives *unake* in face of Tam. *ulakkei*, Gondi *uskāl*, Toda *wask-* "pestle." If the connection were proved it would be most probable that *phala* was borrowed from Dravidian. But "fruit" is called in Khmer *phlĕ*, in Kaseng *plĕi*, in Bahnar *pleĭ*, in Stieng *plĕi*; and Prof. Przyluski who communicates these words to me adds that, in his opinion, they could not have been borrowed from India, because Annamite, in which there is no Indian influence, has *trai* which goes back to *blai* attested in the 17th century by Father Rhodes.

It is very curious that the same problem arises about a word which is the name neither of an animal nor a plant, nor the name of any ~~ordinary~~ article. Of the ancient Indo-European word for "mouth" occurring in the Ṛgveda under the forms, *ās-*, *āsan-*, *ās(i)ya*, there remains no trace to-day except in the dialects of the mountainous regions of the North-West (*cf.* Grierson, *Piś. Lang.*, p. 75 ; and the lists of the *Ling. Survey*, No. 36). Besides this word and the mysterious *práty ānám* I, 52, 15, 37 (from which the word *ānīkam* "face" is derived) the Ṛgveda offers some examples of a new word *múkha*—, the use of which appears to have been already current: it is applied to the author of a hymn IV, 39, 6 ; to Agni VIII, 43, 10 (*cf. Viçvátomukha*, I, 97, 6 ; X, 81, 3) ; to the Puruṣa X, 90, 11 ; it designates the point of the arrow VI, 75, 15 ; in a comparatively late hymn I, 162, 2 *mukhataḥ* is translated "by the bridle"; which presupposes that *mukha* was used for the mouth of the horse. Whence comes this word which is used everywhere in Indo-Aryan to-day (except in Sindhi in which there is a representative of *Vaktra-*) and which ~~the~~ Afghan ~~has borrowed~~ (*max*) ? The Indo-European words which are usually referred to, Lette *mute* Got. *munþs*, old High German *mūla* (and even Skr. *mūla-* "root" if the conjecture of Prof. Wackernagel is accepted. *Sitzber. Berlin*, 1918, p. 410) are of known formation ; but one would search in vain for *-kha-* amongst the normal suffixes in Sanskrit (*mayūkha-* "nail," "peg" is solitary and recalls modern Iranian, Persian *mēx*, etc. [See the works of P. Horn, and Hübschmann under No. 1005] without it being possible to propose a common ancient form).

Now, if we admit that Indo-European of India had any derivative of original **mu-* then its deformation might be attributed to local influences. By a still simpler process, the old word *ās* might have been replaced by a popular form borrowed from the native tribes. One will therefore, be inclined to accept with slight modification, the identification already proposed by Gundert and Kittel of *mukha-* with the Dravidian words for "nose." Can. *mūgu* along with *mū*, Tel. *mukku*, Tam. *mūkku*, Gondi, *massor*, Malto *musoth*, Brahui *bāmus* (where *bā* is the Dravidian term for "mouth"; see the list of *Linguistic Survey*, No. 36; for the words for "nose," No. 34), Kui *mungēli*[1]; these names appear to be authentic because they are connected with all the words expressing the idea of "in front" (Can. Tel. *mũ*, Tam. *mun* Kur. *mund*—, Brah. *mōn* "in front," Can. *mūti*. "face, mouth," Toda *mūn* "face," Tam. *mullal*, Kur. *muddh* "first" etc.). That the term for "mouth" or "face" would be subject to renewal, is not at all astonishing; *mukha-* itself has in modern Indo-Aryan another rival in: Mar. *toṇḍ*, Guj. Beng. *tuṇḍ*, Singh. *tuḍa tola*; this word was previously applied to animals; in Pali and in Sanskrit *tuṇḍa*— designates "trunk, beak, snout"; it is evidently the same as Tam. *tuṇḍi* "beak," Gondi *tuḍḍi* "mouth, face"; probably Malto *toroth* "mouth" (on the contrary Tel. *toṇḍamu* "trunk" appears to be a loan word, and Can. *tuṭi* "lips" recalls too much Beng. *thomṭ*, deformation of the term for "lips," Mar. etc. *oṭh*, Skr. *oṣṭha-* to be taken into consideration).

In the first place, therefore, the probabilities would stand for *mukha-* being a loan word from Dravidian.

[1] It is curious that Kāçmiri *muk* means "short and flat (nose)" while Skr. *mūka-* (Mar. *mukā* etc.) "dumb" is related to the family of Gr. *μυχός*, Arm. *munǰ*, Lat. *mūtus*.

In such a case one would be convinced that Dravidian had certainly, as the history of *ghoṭa-* made us suspect, aspirate occlusive ; and hence one would be justified in suggesting new equivalences for

But it is not confirmed that *mukha-* comes from Dravidian. Let us consult the Munda lists of the Linguistic Survey. On the one hand the North-Eastern group gives for "mouth" a word *mocā* ; we cannot say in the present state of our knowledge if it has anything to do with Vedic *mukha-* but it curiously reminds us of the modern names of "moustache" in two other families : H. *mūñchī mucē*, Mar. *mis*, and Can. *mīse*, Tam. *mīcai*. On the other hand, the word for nose is everywhere *mu* or *mū* ; and Prof. Sten Konow has pointed out in his Introduction, p. 13, that Bahnar has *muh* ; and Prof. Przyluski communicates to me the following list : Khmer *cramuh*, Stieng *trömuh*, Annamite *mui* (the substitution of *i* for an ancient final is regular in Annamite), Môn and Bahnar *muh*, Sedang *moh*, and lastly Čuru and Semang (the last of the Malaya Peninsula) *muk* which very likely preserves the most ancient form. We can scarcely see how to classify all these forms. Besides,

[1] For instance modern Indo-Aryan (Gypsy included) *-phir-* "turn, change," is of unknown etymology (what is said in *Langue Marathe* p. xii, and in the erratum on p. 131 is hardly more satisfactory than before). There might be relation between Can. *pera*, Gondi *pijja* "behind, in the back" (Can. *pera tege* "to draw back." "to come back"), Tel. *peraḍu* "~~[illegible] of the back~~, Tam. *pira*, Tel. *pere*, Brahui *pēn* "other" (Brah. *pèr*, "roll up" must be rather related to Kur. *pes* "pick up"). Of course there exists in Tibetan an adverb *phyir* "newly, re—," but Prof. Przyluski falls back on Lepcha *byil* "recommence" and other analogous forms, and suggests that a root *bal* or *byal* meaning "to repeat" must have been at the basis.

it is good to bear in mind that at the root there is an onomatopoeic word, on account of which the agreements are possible. One knows indeed the difficulties presented by the etymology of the words like Gr. *μῦθος*, Lat. *mūgiō*, *mūtus*, French *museau*, etc.

The conclusions which are drawn from all that has been said and which it is necessary to formulate in order to oppose a tendency to which one has been tempted hitherto to yield too easily are above all negative. In the present state of our knowledge, there is nothing which permits us to affirm that the aspect assumed by Aryan in India is due to its adoption by a population speaking Dravidian languages. If there is any substratum at all, it can be searched for equally well in other families, especially in Munda.

On the other hand the vocabularies furnish a proof of very ancient relations between the populations speaking Sanskrit and Dravidian. But in what did these relations consist: superposition and substitution from Sanskrit to Dravidian, direct contact or indirect exchanges? It is impossible to determine that. So far as there is a chronology of the Sanskrit texts these relations can be dated at the earliest by the end of the Vedic period and would be localised at first in Northern India. One would like to ascertain which dialects Dravidian or Indo-Aryan, were involved in it: unfortunately the evidences are confusing. The initial *b*- of *biḍāla* confirmed by Kāçmiri and Syrian Gypsy is to-day in Dravidian the characteristic of the Canara-Kurukh-Brahui group; the *v* of *Vījana-vyajana*- (if the interpretation suggested above is taken into consideration) characterises the Telugu-Gondi-Tamil group; as the division of *b* and *v* between the Western and Eastern dialects in Dravidian corresponds with that in Aryan, one could say that here is a proof of the two ways of exchange: it is possible, because these loans do not count among the most ancient ones. On the other hand the name of the "peacock," for instance, would give the occasion for a discussion on the alteration *l* : *r*; but it has been seen that Eastern Munda contradicts Dravidian.

Perhaps the principal interest for ourselves in the study of ancient loans (and it would be necessary to try both ways since Dravidian has borrowed much from Aryan) would be to form an idea of prehistoric Dravidian; because even those Dravidian languages which have a past are only attested in a definite way, for the first time, a few centuries after the Christian Era. Moreover the complications we have met with, suggest that Dravidian like Sanskrit may have taken loans of vocabulary from Munda, which must be at least as ancient as Dravidian in India. As far as the borrowings made by Sanskrit are concerned, we have seen that the notions formed up till now are to be either revised or further defined and with the advancement of research new snares and problems do arise. If it is no reason for giving up this research it is one for bringing into it much caution and for leaving necessary room for possibilities to which hitherto too little attention has been paid.

## PART III

# PRE-ARYAN AND PRE-DRAVIDIAN IN INDIA

BY

SYLVAIN LEVI

# Pre-Aryan and Pre-Dravidian in India[1]

The geographical nomenclature of ancient India presents a certain number of terms constituting almost identical pairs, differentiated between themselves only by the nature of their initial consonants. I propose to examine some of them here.

1. *Kosala-Tosala.*—The name of Kosala is familiar to the Sanskrit epics. The Rāmāyaṇa begins with the eulogy of the country of Kosala, on the banks of the Sarayū; Daśaratha, the father of Rāma, is king of the country of Kosala; the mother of Rāma is Kausalyā "the Kosalian"; the city of Ayodhyā, the capital of the kingdom of Kosala, is commonly designated as Kosalā. The Mahābhārata often mentions the people and the city; it associates the Kosalans with Kāśi, Matsya, Karūṣa, Cedi, and Puṇḍra. In the accounts connected with the life and the teaching of Buddha, Kosala also occupies a great place; it is the most important kingdom of Northern India; the King Prasenajit, the contemporary of Buddha, has his capital at Śrāvastī. The name of Kosala goes back even to the Vedic times; it is mentioned, in association with Videha, in the Śatapatha Brāhmaṇa, I, 4, i, 17. Of the Kosalans, the Mahābhārata distinguishes those of the East (Pūrva°, Prāk°) and those of the North (Uttara°); the Rāmāyaṇa distinguishes those of the North (Uttara°) as the Kosalans *par*

[1] Journal Asiatique, Tome cciii (1923), pp. 1-57,

*excellence* (VII, 107, 7). Later on, Kosala proper (Kośala-deśa) or Great Kośala (Mahā°) received the designation of Southern Kośala (Dakṣiṇa°); it is under this name that Kosala is frequently mentioned in the epigraphy of the Middle ages. While the Northern Kosala is the country of Oudh to the North of the Ganges, the Southern Kosala extends on one side up to Berar and Orissa and on the other up to Amarakantak and Bastar. The region of Chhattisgarh along the upper course of the Mahānadi is its nucleus.

The name of Tosala has not acquired the same celebrity as that of Kosala. It is met with, coupled with the name of Kosala and probably saved from oblivion through the prestige of its twin, in *Atharva-Veda Pariśiṣṭa*, Chap. 56, in a list of people connected with the South-East; the Kosala of this passage is, therefore, Dakṣiṇa-Kośala; it appears in the same way in the geographical lists of some of the Purāṇas (*Matsya P.* 113, 53; *Mārkaṇḍeya P.* 57, 54 -*Vāyu P.* 45, 133: Tośalāḥ Kośalāḥ); it is still the same even in the curious *résumé* of Indian geography introduced by Vāgbhaṭa in the commentary on his art of Poetry (*Kāvyānuśāsana*, ed. Kāvyamālā, p. 4, 4): *Vārāṇasyāḥ parataḥ pūrvadeśaḥ! Yatr Aṅga Kaliṅga Kosala Tosala-Otkala*........; Hemacandra has reproduced the same list in his treatise on the same subject, which bears the same title (*Kāvyānuśāsana*, ed. Kāvyamālā, adhy. 3, p. 127). Tosala or Tosalaka, "the native of Tosala," is the name of a wrestler vanquished by Kṛṣṇa (*Harivaṁśa*, II, 30, 50; 48; 55; *Viṣṇupurāṇa*, tran. Wilson[2], Vol. V, p. 39). Tosaliputra, Prakrit Tosalīputta, "the son of the Tosalian," is a Jaina Ācārya, who was the teacher of Ārya Rakṣita or Rakṣitasvāmin, disciple and successor of Vajra, the last of the Daśapūrvin

(*Āvaśyaka -nijjutti* 8, in *Ind. Stud.*, XVII, 63; Hemacandra, *Pariśiṣṭaparvan*, XIII, 38). The name of Tosalī (in the feminine) is hardly known to Indianists except from the inscriptions of Aśoka; two of the different edicts, of Dhauli, are addressed to the Kumārá and the Mahāmātras at Tosalī (*Tosaliyaṁ Mahāmāta nagaraviyahālaka*, 1; *Tosaliyaṁ Kumāle Mahāmātā ca*, 2). The name of Tosalī must have been applied to a region, because we find the mention of Northern Tosalī (Uttara-Tosalī) and Southern Tosalī (Dakṣiṇa-Tosalī); the King of Orissa Śubhakaradeva, who reigned towards the end of the 8th century, ~~while presenting~~ to the Emperor of China his own copy of the *Gaṇḍavyūha* in 795, issues a document conveying the gift from Uttara-Tosalī (*Ep. Ind.*, XV, p. 3). A deed of gift by Śivarāja in 283 (Gupta) *i.e.*, 601 A.D. (*Ep. Ind.*, IX, 286), discovered at Patiakella, mentions Dakṣiṇa-Tosalī in a rather obscure context, either as the residence of his suzerain, which is the way the editor of the inscription, Mr. Banerji, takes it or as the district in which Vortanoka whence the document issues, was situated. Both of these documents have been discovered in Orissa in the district of Cuttack. It is also in this district that Dhauli is situated at a distance of 4 miles South-South-West of Bhuvaneśvar; the inscriptions of Aśoka are engraved there on a rock called Aswastama, near the summit of a low hill. It is therefore evident that Tosalī occupied almost the same site as that of the Dhauli of to-day. There is no accounting for the indication furnished by Ptolemy who places Tōsalei or Tōsalē in India beyond the Ganges, at 150° East and 23° 20′ North, on the way from the Ganges to the peninsula of Gold (Khrusē Khersonēsos), in the vicinity of the Kirāta (Kirrhadia, Tiladai), in the centre of a region which corresponds to modern Sylhet and Manipur. To add to our confusion, Ptolemy places at 5° South and 4° East of Tōsalei, a city called Trilingon or Triglypton, which he qualifies as βασι'λειον "the royal residence," and which may very well be Triliṅga, of which we shall have to speak later on, a region situated in fact to the South of Tosalī, rather to the South-South-West, along the Western coast of the Bay of Bengal, in cis-Gangetic India according to the division adopted by Ptolemy. The other towns enumerated by Ptolemy in the same paragraph have not yet been identified: Rhandamarkotta, where there is an abundance of nard; Athēna gouṛon, Maniaina (Maniataia), Tōsalei, Alosanga, Adeisaga, Kimara, Parisara, Tougma which is a capital (metropolis), etc. For the first of these names a suggestion may be offered *en passant*, which may lead to its definite identification by discarding at any rate all the previous identifications which McCrindle has summarised in an important note (*Ind. Ant.*, XIII, 382). "Rhadamarkotta (v. l. Rhandamarkotta). Saint Martin has identified this with Raṅgâmaṭî, an ancient capital situated on the western bank of the lower Brahmaputra, and now called Udêpur (Udayapura,—*city of Sunrise*). Yule who agrees with this identification, gives as the Sanskrit form of the name of the place, Rangamṛtika. The passage about *Nard* which follows the mention of Rhadamarkotta in the majority of editions is, according to Saint Martin (*Étude*, p. 352 and note), manifestly corrupt. Some editors correct πολλη', *much*, into πο'λεις, *cities*, and thus Nardos becomes the name of a town, and Rhadamarkotta the name of a district to which Nardos and the towns that come after it in the table belong. On this point we may quote a passage from Wilford, whose views regarding Rhadamarkotta were different. He says

(*Asiat. Research*, Vol. XIV, p. 441), 'Ptolemy has delineated tolerably well the two branches of the river of Âvâ and the relative situation of two towns upon them, which still retain their ancient, name, only they are transposed. These two towns are Urathêna, and Nardos or Nardon; Urathena is Rhâdana, the ancient name of Amarapur, and Nøadon is Nartenh on the Kayn-dween......' He says that 'Nartenh was situated in the country of Rhandamarkoṭa, literally, the Fort of Randamar, after which the whole country was desigtated.' All the exegetists appear to me to have gone wrong; Wilford, however, had a glimpse of one part of the solution. The Sanskrit name of nard is *nalada*; a metathesis, always easy in the case of *r* in Sanskrit, has given rise to *lan* (*a*) *da* and then *randa*. It may be as well noted that the aspirate which accompanies the initial *r* of *rhando*° or *rhado*° is a purely Greek feature, and does not imply any aspiration in the original word. As to the alternation of *l* and *r* in the name of nard we have a sure trace in the gaṇa *kisarādi* on Pāṇini, IV, 4, 53; the grammarian prescribes that for designating the merchants of certain perfumes one must have a derivation in *ika* from the name of the perfume. The gaṇapāṭha gives immediately after *Kisara* the words *narada* and *nalada*; Böhtlingk, P.W², under *narada*, does not hesitate to recognise in it the name of nard. I find that Candragomin in the corresponding gaṇa (ad III, 4, 55) has omitted *narada* and retained only *nalada*. Thus the annotation which accompanies the name of the locality in Ptolemy is occasioned by the name itself, which it explains. I do not know how one should restore the final syllables. The *nalada* in botanica nomenclature is Nardostachys Jatamansi or Nardus Indicus; Khory and Katrak (*Materia*, II, 344) indicate the alpine Himālaya as its habitat; Yule and Burnell likewise (*Hobson-Jobson*, under *nard*) indicate that the plant Nardostachys Jatamansi is "a native of the loftier Himālaya." If Rhandamarkotta abounds in nard, it must, therefore, be situated either in the Himalayan heights or must be in such a vicinity as to be able to serve the market. Rhandamarkotta, therefore, leads us towards upper Bengal; we may ask what error of information could have led Ptolemy to locate Tosalī (Tōsalei, Tōsalē) and Triliṅga (Triliṅgon) to the east of the Ganges. And yet Ptolemy was not ignorant of the importance of Tosalī, for he has himself termed it a capital (metropolis).

However that may be it remains certain that Tosalī was situated in the district of Cuttack, in Orissa, and that the present village of Dhauli stands on a site near to, or identical with that of Tosalī. It can be then asked whether the very name of Dhauli does not represent the ancient name Tosalī; the two names sound so strangely alike that mere chance seems out of the question. The transformation of Tosalī into Dhauli is not a phonetic impossibility. The intervocalic sibilant of Sanskrit can, and in certain cases must become a simple aspirate in Prākrits (Pischel, 264), for example *diaha*=*divasa* and still better *dūhala* beside *dūsara* "unfortunate" =*duḥsara*. If Tosalī could likewise develop into Tohalī,[1] this unintelligible name could suggest Dhauli "the white." Nevertheless, it must be admitted that the widening of the intervocalic *s* is frequent only in the North-Western group: Sindhi, Panjābi, Kāshmiri; it

[1] Let me point out, without any intention of drawing any argument from it, that Varāha Mihira, *Bṛh. S*, XIV, 27, classes amongst the populations of the North, beside the *Hūṇa*, the Kohala for which the commentator Ūtpala substitutes Kośala.

is already rarer in Gujrāti and in Rājputānā (Jules Bloch *Langue Marathe*, § 160). But the phonetics of place-names leave the gate widely open to fancy.

A text which has not yet been mentioned will perhaps help the solution of the problem of the site of Tosalī; I have found it in the Gaṇḍavyūha. The Gandavyūha is a Sanskrit-Buddhist work preserved in Nepal and not yet published. Rāj. Mitra has given an analysis of it in his catalogue, *The Sanskrit-Buddhist Literature of Nepal*, p. 90. Its extent is considerable. In reality, however, it is only a fragment; it forms the last part of the vast collection which bears the title of Avataṁsaka, the entirety of which is preserved in the Chinese and Tibetan versions. On account of its importance the Avataṁsaka has been, on two occasions, completely translated into Chinese under the direction of Buddhabhadra between 398 and 421; and under the direction of Śikṣānanda between 695 and 699. The section which forms the Gaṇḍavyūha has been translated a third time into Chinese by Prājña, between 796 and 798, from a manuscript which had been sent to the Emperor of China by King Subhakaradeva of Orissa; the official letter which accompanied this present has been translated at the end of the work. Thus we know that the last section of the Avataṁsaka was already treated as a separate work in the 8th century in Orissa and that it was in special favour there at that time. Also about this time, Śāntideva repeatedly cites the Gaṇḍavyūha, by this very name, in his Śikṣāsamuccaya; it is even with a quotation from the Gaṇḍavyūha that this treatise begins.

The Gaṇḍavyūha was well calculated to gain popularity. For his exposition of the Mahāyānist theology, the author has succeeded in devising an ingenious and striking framework which could not fail to attract the reader. The hero of the work Sudhana is a favourite disciple of Mañjuśrī who, under the direction of his preceptor, makes circuit of India, stage by stage, seeking lessons now from a king, now from a slave, from ancient sage or from innocent children. After having instructed him as much as she could, the Upāsikā Acalasthirā said to him: "Now young man, go on your way; in this Dekkhan where we are, there is the country of Amita-Tosala; in that country there is a city called Tosala; there dwells a wandering monk of the name of Sarvagāmin."...He, therefore, went away to this country of Amita-Tosala, to search for the city of Tosala and he reached the city of Tosala by stages. At the time of sunset, he entered the city of Tosala; he stopped in the middle of the city square, and then from lane to lane, from place to place and from cart-road to cart-road, at last he found Sarvagāmin and when the night was drawing to its end, he perceived to the north of the city of Tosala, the mountain called Surabha of which the summit was covered with lawns, bowers of trees, plants, groves, and gardens.

The Chinese translations present singular divergences on the points which interest us here. The most ancient translator Buddhabhadra (ed., Tokyo, I, 9, 43[a]) gives to the *Amita-Tosala* of the Sanskrit text the name of *pu ko tch'eng* [1] which is, according to the Mahāvyutpatti, 246, 116 and 247, 123, the equivalent of *atulya* "incomparable"; if need be this meaning can be derived from *Amita*, literally "un-measured, without measure," but the normal

不可稱

translation of the word *Amita* in Chinese is *wu leang*[1] which, in fact, can be found in the traslations of Sikṣānanda (I, 4, 28[a]) and Prājña (I, 5, 52[b]). Sikṣānanda and Prājña transcribe the name of the town as *tu-sa-lo*[2]; Buddhabhadra translates it by *tche-tsu*[3] which serves as equivalent to the word *saṁtuṣṭa* "satisfied" in Mahāvyutpatti, 145, 9. Buddhabhadra thought he recognised in the name of Tosala the root *tuṣ* "to satisfy"; in fact, the Sanskrit manuscripts of the Gaṇḍavyūha, which I have examined, contain in the text of this single passage the three alternative forms: Tosala, Toṣala and even Tosara. Buddhabhadra does not give the name of the mountain; he only says: "To the north of this city, there is a mountain which shines as bright as the rising sun." Śikṣānanda and Prājña agree quite unexpectedly in locating the mountain to the "east of the city;" both of them translate the name in Chinese; Śikṣānanda gives *shen tö*[4] "good virtue" which presupposes a Sanskrit form *suguṇa*, Prājña translates as *miao ki siang*[5] "marvellous auspices" which is one of the equivalents of the name of Mañjuśrī. It appears that on this point of local onomastic, the official manuscript of the king of Orissa, which served as the basis of Prājña's translation must be believed. An enquiry on the spot perhaps will settle the question.

It may be observed that most of the proper names belonging to the type which we have under consideration have never attained a stable and constant form in writing

[1] 無量 [2] 都薩羅 [3] 知足

[4] 善德 [5] 妙吉祥

their appearance has always an aspect which disconcerts the scribe. The dental sibilant of the words *Kosala* and *Tosala*, preserved in the middle in spite of the vowel *o* is a sort of defiance of the rigorous laws of Sanskrit grammar which enjoins in such cases the modification of the dental (*s*) into the cerebral (*ṣ*). The form *Kośala*, with a palatal sibilant has also been adopted for general use; this had the advantage of avoiding the difficulty; it had still more appreciable advantage of connecting this embarrassing ethnic with a family of common words, *Kośa*, *Kuśa*, *Kuśala*, which contain the palatal sibilant. *Tosala* has been no less affected; it has been attracted by the analogies of the words *toṣa*, etc., which express satisfaction; we have therefore more often *Toṣala*, but sometimes *Tośala* also as *Kośala*.

2. *Aṅga-Vaṅga.*—These two names are so familiar throughout Sanskrit literature that they hardly need explanation. Aṅga is already mentioned in *Atharva-Veda*, V, 22, 14 by the side of Magadha, as the eastern limit of the Aryan world. Vaṅga (Baṅga) still survives in the name of Bengal (=Baṅga+āla). Aṅga and Vaṅga, most often coupled together, have ordinarily as their companion Kaliṅga to which we shall return presently. All three, with Puṇḍra (and Suhma), which we shall also have to consider, are represented (*Mahābhārata*, I, 104) as five brothers born for the benefit of King Bali, from a union accomplished, at his request, between the queen Sudeṣṇā and the blind old ṛṣi Dīrghatamas; the whole chapter has such a singular scent of savagery that the Indian translator, the author of the English version published by P. C. Roy, has been obliged several times to take recourse to Latin for the sake of decency. Here we are doubtless confronted by old local legends which

the study of folklore will discover in the Austro-Asiatic domain. Aṅga and Vaṅga had long remained suspect to the Aryans of India. Baudhāyana, so rich in curious features, prescribes (I, 2, 14) a sacrifice of expiation after a travel amongst the Āraṭṭa, the Kāraskara, the Puṇḍra, the Sauvīra, the Vaṅga, the Kaliṅga, and the Prānūna. (*Āraṭṭān Kāraskarān Puṇḍrān Sauvīrān Vaṅga-Kaliṅgān Prānūnān iti ca gatvā punastomena yajeta sarvapṛṣṭhayā vā*). It will be noticed that Vaṅga and Kaliṅga are united in a compound noun while the other peoples are mentioned one by one. In the stanza which precedes this one Baudhāyana had related a verse which classes the Aṅga amongst the halfbreeds: *Avantayo'ṅga Magadhāḥ Surāṣṭrā Dakṣiṇāpathāḥ | Upāvṛt Sindhusauvīrā ete saṁkīrṇayonayaḥ*. The very reasons which attributed to these countries a bad reputation in the Brāhmaṇical society assured them a privileged rank in the heretical churches. For the Jainas, Aṅga is almost a holy land; Campā, the capital, is the residence of a large number of holy personages of Jain legend and history. The Bhagavatī places Aṅga and Vaṅga at the head of a list of sixteen peoples, before the Magadha (Weber, *Ind. St.*, XVI, 304). One of the Upāṅgas, the Prajñāpanā, classes Aṅga and Vaṅga in the first group of Ārya peoples whom it calls the *Khettāriya*; the list begins thus: *Rāyagiha Magaha, Campā Aṁgā taha, Tāmalitti Vaṅga ya* (*ibid*, p. 397). Buddhism incorporates Aṅga in the classical list of sixteen kingdoms; Vaṅga occupies an inferior position. The Aṅguttara-nikāya makes mention of it only once (I, 213) in the list of sixteen kingdoms; everywhere else the place is occupied by the Vaṁsa (Sansk. Vatsa); the later Buddhist literature constantly put together Aṅga and

Vaṅga. Aṅga corresponds to the district of Bhagalpur and Vaṅga to the districts of Birbhum, Murshidabad, Burdwan, and Nadiya in Bengal.

3. *Kaliṅga-Triliṅga*—"Kaliṅga comprised all the Eastern coast between the Utkalas, on the north and the Teliṅgas on the south. The Vaitaraṇī flowed through it; the Mahendra mountains (the Eastern Ghats) were within its southern limits. Kaliṅga comprised therefore, the modern province of Orissa, the district of Ganjam and probably also that of Vizagapatam." (Pargiter, *Mark. P.*, p. 334). We have just seen the close relationship which binds Kaliṅga with Aṅga and Vaṅga, and the nature of the reprobation which they received in common from the Brāhmaṇical schools. Kaliṅga had even the honour of having a special verse devoted to it in the code of Baudhāyana, a traditional verse which the legislator adopts on his own account (I, 2, 15): "The adage is cited: it is to commit a sin with the legs to go to Kaliṅga; for its atonement, the saints prescribe a Vaiśvānara libation (*atrāpy udāharanti, padbhyām sa kurute pāpaṁ yaḥ Kaliṅgān prapadyate । ṛṣayo niṣkṛtim tasya prāhur vaiśvānaraṁ haviḥ*). The juristic compilations of the last centuries continue to register, as an echo of this reprobation, another traditional verse: "If one goes to Aṅga, Vaṅga, Kaliṅga, Saurāṣṭra and Magadha except for a pilgrimage, it is necessary for him to receive a new sacrament."

*Aṅga Vaṅga Kaliṅgeṣu Saurāṣṭre Magadheṣu ca । tīrthayātrāṁ vinā gacchan punaḥ saṁskāram arhati* (cited by R. P. Chanda, Sir Asutosh Volumes, III, 1, 10, 7).

Regarding Kaliṅga the Mahābhārata presents a curious hesitation in course of the same canto, at an interval of some verses in VIII, 44, 2066; the Kaliṅgas are enumerated amongst the tribes whose religion is bad (*durdharma*), pêle-mêle with the Kāraskara, the Māhiṣaka, the Kerala, the Karkoṭaka, and the Vīraka; but in VIII, 45, 2084, they are counted amongst peoples who know the eternal law (*dharmaṁ jānanti śāsvatam*) in the company of the nations who are the highest of Brahmanism, Kuru, Pañcāla, Sālva, Matsya, Naimiṣa, etc. This change of attitude is undoubtedly due to the importance held by Kaliṅga since the time when the Indian civilisation spread along the Bay of Bengal. We know that the conquest of Kaliṅga, at the cost of streams of blood, provoked the moral crisis from which the Emperor Aśoka came out transformed. After him, under Khāravela, Kaliṅga became the centre of a powerful empire of which the chief assumed the title of Cakravartin. Buddhism had one of its holy places in Kaliṅga: this was the capital of the country, Dantapura, "the city of the tooth" whence the holy relic was later on transported to Ceylon. Pliny mentions on several occasions the Calingae (VI, 18; 19; 20). Ptolemy enumerates a city of Kalliga (VII, i, 93) amongst the Maisôloi, between the Kistna and the Godavari. Kalingapatam, port of the district of Ganjam, still preserves the old name of the region. The appellation of Kling, applied to the Indians of all origin all through the Malayan world, attests the brilliant rôle of the men of Kalinga in the diffusion of the Indian civilisation in the Far East. (See *Hobson-Jobson*, under *Kling*).

The term symmetrical to Kaliṅga appears in the written documents only at a later date; it takes diverse forms which present the terrible perplexity of the scribes in face of a kind of monster. The *P. W.* records the forms *Triliṅga* and *Tailaṅga*; the Mārkaṇḍeya P., 58, 28 and the Vāyu

P., 45, 111 write: *Tilaṅga*. We find in the inscriptions also *Tiliṅga* (*Ep. Ind.*, XIV, 90), *Telunga* (*ibid*, XIV, 271), *Tiriliṅga* (*ibid*, XIV, 361), *Trikaliṅga* (*ibid*, XII, 208 and *pass.*). The Arab and Persian authors write *Tilang, Tiliṅg, Tiliṅgana*; in the nomenclature of the languages of India, the language of this country is called *Telugu*. An inscription of the 14th century thus traces the limits of the country: "To the West and to the East, two famous countries, Mahārāṣṭra and Kaliṅga; to the South and to the North, Pāṇḍya and Kanyakubja; it is that country which is called Tiliṅga" (*paścāt purastād yasya deśau khyātau Mahārāṣṭra-Kaliṅga-saṃjñau* | *avāg udak Pāṇḍyaka Kanyakubjau deśas sa tatrāsti Tiliṅganāma*. Sriraṅgam Plates, Saka 1280 in *Ep. Ind.*, XIV, 90). The region thus defined covers the greatest part of eastern India According to the notice on the Telugu in the *Linguistic Survey*, Vol. IV, p. 577, "The Telugu country is bounded towards the East by the Bay of Bengal from Barwa in the Ganjam district in the north to near Madras in the South. From Barwa the frontier line goes westwards through Ganjam to the Eastern Ghats and then South-westwards crosses the Sabari on the border of the Sunkam and Bijji Taluks in the State of Bastar, and thence runs along the range of Bela Dila to the Indrāvati; it follows this river to its confluence with the Godavari, and then runs through Chanda cutting off the southern part of that district and farther eastwards, including the southern border of the district of Wun. It then turns southwards to the Godavari, as its confluence with the Mānjira, and thence farther south towards Bidar, when Telugu meets with Kanarese. The frontier line between the two forms of speech then runs almost due south through the dominions of the Nizam. The Telugu country further occupies the north-eastern edge of Bellary, the greater eastern part of Anantapur, and the eastern corner of Mysore. Through North Arcot and Chingleput the border line thence runs back to the sea." If the Telugu country has such an extension, one understands why Tārānātha (p. 264) designates Kaliṅga as merely a part of Triliṅga. But on the other hand it is astonishing that the name of the country is not met with till a late period, only after the year 1000 A.D. By a singular anomaly Ptolemy is the only guarantee of the name for all the earlier period. He records the city of *Trilingon*, the royal residence which he places in the trans-Gangetic India (VII, 2, 23), at 154° East × 18° North; the city is also called *Triglypton* (var. *Triglyphon*); in the region where it is situated, "it is said, adds Ptolemy, that the cocks are bearded, the crows and the parrots are white." If the white parrots refer to the cockatoos, which is very probable, the indication can only point to the further regions of the Far East, as "the cockatoos are confined to the Australian region, to the Philippines, and Sulu; the cockatoo galerita which is completely white is peculiar to Australia and Tasmania." (*Cambridge Natural History*, Vol. IX, *Birds*, p. 372.) The white crows lead in another direction altogether; if they refer to the species called *Dendrocitta leucogastra*, which "has the top of the head, the neck, the breastbone, the abdomen and the covering of the tail white, the species belongs to south India, particularly to Malabar (*Fauna of British India, Birds*, I, p. 31). We would be thus brought back to India and to the very borders of the Telugu country. However, the place assigned to Trilingon on the map of Ptolemy is very far from there; it is located in modern Arakan, in the interior of the land, on the heights of Akyab. The name would not be unexpected there, because it is still preserved in that region under the form of *Talaing*. It is known that the Burmese designated under this name the Mōn race which had preceded them in Pegu and disseminated there a civilisation, tributary to India. According to Sir Arthur Phayre, it can be generally admitted that Talaing = Telinga: Forchhamer has proposed to replace this interpretation by another explanation drawn from the Mōn language where *talaiṅg* signifies "trampled over by feet;" the derogatory term might have replaced the proper ethnical name of the Mōns after their defeat (*cf. Hobson-Jobson*, s. v. *Talaing* for the texts and the references). Phayre himself notes that though Kalinga figures in the Peguan annals, "the word Telingāna is never met with there." The case is therefore exactly parallel to that of India; we have before us a name of very ancient aspect, which the literature has ignored for a long time. It is possible, even probable, that the literary usage has preferred to maintain the old denomination of Andhra, applied by Brahmanism since the Vedic times (Aitareya Brāhmaṇa), and consecrated by its mere antiquity, rather than to employ a vocable of uncertain form. The other name given to Trilingon in Ptolemy, Triglypton or Triglyphon, appears to be an attempt at interpretation, conforming to that which the medieval usage in India had already furnished. The term is composed of *tri* = Sk. *tri* "three" + *glypton* or *glyphon*, both of which has the meaning of "chiselled and engraved," the "triglyph" (*triglyphos* or *triglyphon*; its gender is undetermined) is a term in architecture which designates a feature of the frieze in the Doric entablature; the triglyph is composed of the parallel grooves grouped by threes, with the "drops" below, represented by the tips of cones, which symbolise drops of water flowing from the roof through the grooves and resting in suspense. Nothing could better recall to a Greek, by a familiar image, the stone liṅga decorated with vertical grooves by which the water of sacred aspersions drop down. Ptolemy's informant had picked up an interpretation which is known even to-day; one continues to explain *Tiliṅga*, etc., still by *Triliṅga* and *Triliṅga* would be the country of three Liṅgas, divine manifestations of Śiva on the three mountains which mark the frontier of the Telugu country, Kāleśvara, Śrīśaila and Bhīmeśvara. Kāleśvara is situated on the Kistna, at the entrance of the pass by which it flows into the plain; Śrīśaila is at the confluence of the Wainganga with the Godavari in the district of Chanda; Bhīmeśvara is in the Western Ghats, at the point where the Telugu country touches the Maratha country and Mysore. In Pliny also we have another evidence of the interpretation Tiliṅga-Triliṅga (Pliny VI, 18 *Insula in Gange est Magnoe amplitudinis gentem continens unam nomine Modogalingam*), if one admits with Campbell (*Grammar of the Teloogoo*, Introd.) that Modogalinga must be analysed as *Modoga + liṅga*; *Modoga* would represent the Telugu *mūḍuga*, poetical form of the word *mūḍu* "three." But Caldwell (*Compar. Grammar*, Introd., p. 32) contests this explanation: the use of *Mūḍuga* would be pedantic, according to him; the only analysis which he would accept is *Modo = Mūḍu* = 3, *galinga = Kaliṅga*, *i. e.* the three Kaliṅgas, the Trikaliṅga of so many epigraphic documents of the middle age.

We have indicated that the position assigned by Ptolemy to "the royal residence of Trilingon," in modern Arakan is not impossible, but we have had already occasion to explain, as regards Tōsalei-Tosalī mentioned in the same list, VII, 2, 23, that Ptolemy had carried by error to the East of the mouths of the Ganges an itinerary really directed towards the South-West of the delta. The question must remain open pending further discoveries.

One is tempted to class side by side with the peoples of Kaliṅga and Tiliṅga the people of Bhuliṅga who are known to us from numerous sources. Pliny, VI, 20 names the Bolingae amongst the series of peoples who succeed one another up the course of the Indus. Ptolemy, VII, 1, 69, places the Bōlingai to the east of the mountain Ouindios (Vindhya) with the cities of Stagabaza or Bastagaza and of Bardaotis, on the right bank of the Sôa, *i.e.*, the Soṇa (Sôn). The Ganapāṭha annexed to the grammar of Pāṇini names on different occasions, the Bhauliṅgi: on II, 4, 59; IV, 1, 41; IV, 1, 173; the rule enunciated in the last sūtra is applied to the constituting elements of the tribe of the Sālvas, and consequently appears in the traditional verse, collected by the Kāśikā and the Candravṛtti (on Candra, II, 4, 103) which enumerates the six sections of the Sālvas:

*Udumbarās Tilakhalā Madrakārā Yugandharāḥ*
*Bhuliṅgāḥ Śaradaṇḍāś ca Sālvāvayava saṁjñitāḥ.*

The Sālvas are well known (*cf.* Pragiter, *Mārk. P.* 349); they inhabited the vicinity of the Kuru and the Trigarta, at the western foot of the Aravalli. And, consequently, in the Rāmāyaṇa G II, 70, 15 the messengers, sent by Vaśiṣṭha to recall Bharata back from the Kekaya country where he was the guest of his maternal uncle, had to traverse at first the long road which went from Ayodhyā towards Kurukṣetra and the Sarasvatī;

they crossed the sacred river, they next passed the river Śaradaṇḍa, and "then entered into the town of Bhuliṅga." The Bengali recension shows here again its superiority over the two others; the Bombay recension, and the Southern recension, II, 68, 16, give the city the name of Kulinga. The name of Kulingā re-appears this time in the feminine, in the two recensions of Bombay and of the South, II, 71, 6, when the poet describes the itinerary of Bharata returning from Kekaya to Ayodhyā; it is there the name of a river which waters the Doab between the Ganges and the Yamunā. The Bengal recension has here an altogether different text. The Mahā Bhārata does not mention Bhuliṅga as an ethnic name; the word appears there to designate a bird which lives on the other side of the Himālayas and of which the cry "mā sāhasam" warns men to move without precipitation, II, 44, 1545. But the edition of the South, II, 67, 28, writes the name of this bird as Kuliṅga. The Bhuliṅga birds are again mentioned in the great epic, XII, 169, 6326, as "the birds of the sea, sons of the mountains" (*sāmudrāḥ parvatodbhavāḥ*). In the corresponding passage, the edition of the South (XII, 168, 9), substitutes for the bhuliṅga the bhāruṇḍa birds.

4. *Utkala-Mekala.*—The two names are connected together as intimately as Aṅga and Vaṅga. The Rāmāyaṇa which mentions them only once IV, 41, 9 B.; 41, 14 G., refers to them together: *Mekalān Utkalāṁś-caiva*, by the side of Kaliṅga: Kṣemendra, in his resumé (*Rām. mañj.*, IV, 234) combines them still more intimately; *Mekalotkalikāḥ*. The Mahā Bhārata does the same, VIII, 22, 882: *Mekalotkalāḥ Kaliṅgāḥ*; elsewhere it juxtaposes them: VI, 9, 348, *Mekalāś cotkalaiḥ saha*;

VII, 4, 12: *Utkalā Mekalāḥ*. Mr. Pargiter in his translation of the Mārkaṇḍeya P. (p. 327) has a note on these two peoples which we will reproduce in full because of the way it seems to anticipate the conclusions which I am endeavouring to disentangle from this examination of the facts. "The *Utkalas* were well-known (though not, often mentioned in the M.-Bh.) and were a rude tribe of very early origin, for they do not appear to have had any close affinities with the races around them, and the Hari-vaṁśa throws their origin back to the fabulous time of Ila (X, 631-2). Their territory reached on the east the R. Kapiśā (*Raghu- V.* IV, 38....and on the west they touched the Mekalas, for the two peoples are coupled together in the M. Bh. and the Rāmāyaṇa and the Mekalas were the inhabitants of the Mekala hills, *i.e.*, the hills bounding Chhattisgarh on the west and north. Northward dwelt the Puṇḍras and southward the Kaliṅgas. Hence Utkala comprised the southern portion of Chuta Nagpur, the northern tributary states of Orissa and the Balasore district. Various derivations have been suggested of the name Utkala but I would only draw attention to some of the above passages where Utkala and Mekala are placed together as if their names possessed something in common." Utkala is still to-day one of the usual designations of Orissa and the language of Orissa is called at will Oṛiyā, Oḍrī or even Utkali (*Ling.-Surv.*, *V*, Part II, p. 367). As the *Survey* states clearly: "the Orissa country is not confined to the division which now bears that name. It includes a portion of the district of Midnapur in the north. ...Oṛiyā is also the language of most of the district of Singhbhum, belonging to the division of Chota Nagpur and of several neighbouring native states which fall politically within the same division. On the west it is the language of the greater parts of the district of Sambalpur and of a small portion of the district of Raipur in the Central Provinces and also of the number of Native states which lie between these districts and Orissa proper."

If the name of Utkala has preserved its vitality, the name of Mekala has survived only as a memory associated with religion. The heights of Mekala give birth to one of the most important rivers of India, the Narmadā, which is second only to the Ganges in point of sanctity. One of her sacred appellations, recorded by Amara and other lexicographers, is *Mekalakanyakā*, "the daughter of the Mekala." But here also the name having no definitely established form has been attracted by the analogy of the common word "*Mekhalā*" "girdle" and the written form oscillates between the two. The commentator on Amara, Sarvānanda authorises both (ad *Am.* I, 10, 31. *Mekalācalaprabhavatvād Mekala kanyakā Mekhalakanyaketi kecit. Yan Mekhalād bhavati Mekhalaśailaputrī iti khakāravān*). The obscurity of the name of Mekala is painfully evident in the edition of the Mahā Bhārata published at Calcutta, in which the name is printed several times as *Melaka*, under the influence of the common word *melā* "fair." The editor can allege for his justification a distant precedent; the translator of the Saddharma-smṛtyupasthāna Sūtra had already substituted *Melaka* for *Mekala* in his Tibetan version, in which he had reproduced too faithfully the fault committed by the scribe of the Sanskrit original; the author of the Chinese version had read and transcribed *Mekhala* with aspiration (*Pour l'Histoire du Rām.*, p. 27). In another passage of the same Sūtra which mentions, in imitation of the Rāmāyaṇa, G. IV, 40, 20 "the river Śoṇa born from the Mekala" (*Mekalaprabhavam Śoṇam*), the Tibetan version writes *Megalati*, the Chinese version *Mecaka* (*ibid*, p. 18). The official geography of British India has collected and saved this ancient name; under the name of Maikal Range it designates the chain of mountains which starts from the sources of the Narmadā (Amarakantak) and extends towards the South-South-West up to the district of Balaghat.

The country of Utkala bears still another name from which the modern appellation of Orissa is derived. *Oṛissa* is Oḍradeśa, "the country of Oḍra." The supposed Sanskrit original given by Mr. Crooke in the second edition of *Hobson-Jobson*, *Oḍrāṣṭra* (*sic*) is monstrous and fantastic. The first forms used by Europeans, *Ulixa*, *Udeza*, *Orisa*, etc., are derived directly from Oḍradeśa. Uṛiyā, the name universally used to-day for the language of Orissa, comes from the same vocable Odra in its most reduced form. As was the case with Teliṅga, we have here again to do with another word of which the written form has never been definitely settled; one finds, even in the same texts, *Uḍra*, *Oḍra*, *Auḍra*, *cf.* for example, for the Mahā Bhārata, the Index of Sörensen under these different words. The form *Uda*, from which come Oriyā and Orissa, is already warranted by the evidence of Chinese transcriptions. Hiuan-tsang transcribes *Wu tch'a*[1] and the annals of the T'ang dynasty do the same and so does the official version of the letter addressed to the emperor of China by king Śubhakara in 795 A.D., with a manuscript of the Gaṇḍavyuha (see *supra*, p. 69). A form with the nasal inserted, *Uṁda*, *Uṇḍa*, is attested by numerous variants in all kinds of texts. Thus MBh., VI, 9, 365,

[1] 烏荼

in the list of the nations of India, C has *Auḍrāḥ Pauṇḍrāḥ*, B reads *Auṁdrā* and the text followed by the translator of P. C. Roy has the same reading (the Aundras, the Paundras); the southern recension reads *Oṇḍrā Mlecchāḥ*; Manu, X, 44, names amongst the degraded Kṣatriyas *Pauṇḍrakāś Coḍa Draviḍāḥ*; such is the text followed by Bühler, but he records in a note that his reading is a correction for *Coṁḍra°* which is given by different manuscripts of the commentator Medhātithi and also by the commentator Kullūka; he adds that the interpretation followed by W. Jones (*ca+uḍa*) is improbable because the particle *ca* is absolutely useless after the first term. However, the constant conjunction of the Pauṇḍras and the Oḍras appears to justify fully Jones' analysis and translation. While the Chinese has *Wu-tch'a* in the *Saddharma-smṛtyupasthāna sūtra* (corresponding to the Rāmāyaṇa G IV, 41, 18, *tathauḍrān*), the Tibetan translator has *coṇḍā*, by a false interpretation of the original *coṇḍāḥ=ca+uṇḍāḥ* (*Pour l'Hist. du Rām.*, pp. 28 and 98).

By the side of the ethnical group *Uḍ(r)a* (*Uṇḍa*) comes to be classed quite naturally the ethnique Puṇḍa, Puṇḍra with its secondary forms Pauṇḍra, Pauṇḍraka, Pauṇḍrika. The *rapprochement* is the more natural in that the two peoples Pauṇḍra and Uḍra occur very frequently together: MBh., III, 51, 1988, *sa Pauṇḍroḍrān*; VI, 9, 365, *Auḍrāḥ* (C. *Auṁḍrāḥ*) *Pauṇḍrāh*, Viṣṇu P. IV, 24, 18, *Kośal-Auḍra-Pauṇḍraka Tāmraliptān*; Bṛhat Saṁhitā, V, 74, *Pauṇḍra-Auḍra-Kaikaya-janān*; etc. On the other hand, a tradition recorded in the Mahā Bhārata (*cf. supra*, p. 72), I, 104, 4219-4221, groups them with Aṅga, Vaṅga, Kaliṅga, Suhma, as the sons born of the queen Sudeṣṇā by the contact of the ṛṣi

Dīrghatamas; the same epic, XIII, 35, 2158, in accord with Manu, X, 44, classes them amidst the Kṣatriyas degraded to the rank of Śūdra. In combining the data furnished by the Mahā Bhārata Mr. Pargiter (*Mārk. P.*, p. 329) concludes that the Puṇḍra, whose boundaries were Kāśī on the north, Aṅga, Vaṅga and Suhma on the north-east and the east, and Oḍra on the southeast, inhabited the territory which forms to-day Chota Nagpur, less its southern portion. The territory of the Puṇḍras must be clearerly distingushed from the country of Puṇḍra-vardhana, which corresponded to the modern district of Rajshahi, between the Ganges and the Brahmaputra.

Chota Nagpur, partly the ancient domain of the Puṇḍras, is still to-day the habitation of the Muṇḍas, specially in the southern and western portions of the district of Ranchi. It is well-known that the name of Muṇḍā has been chosen by Max Müller to designate a family of languages which have been strongly influenced by the Dravidian, but which are originally independent, and related to the Mōn-Khmêr family and the dialects of the savage tribes of the Malaya peninsula. According to Mr. Risley, *Linguistic Survey*, Vol. IV, p. 79, "The name Muṇḍā is of Sanskrit origin. It means headmen of a village, and is a titular or functional designation used by the members of the tribe, as well as by outsiders, as a distinctive name much in the same way as the Santals call themselves Māñjhī, the Bhumij Sardār; and the Khambu of the Darjiling hills Jimdār." I do not know for what reasons Mr. Risley says that the word "Muṇḍa" is of Sanskrit origin. The word *Muṇḍa* certainly exists in Sanskrit; there it signifies "one whose head is completely shaved." As an ethnic the name appears very rarely in the literature. Only one of the passages where the name is found in the Mahā Bhārata appears really to refer to the Muṇḍa: VI, 56, 2410, the poet describes the order of battle adopted by Bhīṣma: on the left wing are the Muṇḍa, with the Kārūṣa, the Vikuñja, the Kaundivṛṣa. Of the peoples, the last two are otherwise unknown: the Kārūṣa on the contrary, appears fairly often (*cf.* Pargiter, *Mārk. P.*, p. 341); they lived to the south of Kāśī and Vatsa, between Cedi and Magadha. Their territory, therefore, covered partly Baghelkhand and Bundelkhand; and towards the south-east bordered the country still occupied by the Muṇḍa. Other passages of the epic where the name of Muṇḍa is met with, III, 51, 1991; VII, 119, 4728-4730 have a quite different signification; they apply to a population of the north-western frontier of India designated by the nickname of "shaved heads," and specially to the Kamboja of the country of Kabul. The Hindus who are bound by their religion to wear a tuft (*cūḍā*) on the top of their head, despised the foreign populations who shaved their whole head; "shaved like a Greek," "shaved like a Kamboja" (*yavanamuṇḍa, Kambojamuṇḍa*) were expressions in vogue from the time of Pāṇini; the Gaṇapāṭha places them at the beginning of the gaṇa *Mayūravyaṁsakādi* on P. 2, 1, 72. The Vāyu P., 45, 123 names the Muṇḍa in its list of the peoples of Eastern India, between Prāgjyotiṣa (north Bengal) and Videha (Tirhut), before Tāmaliptaka (Tamluk on the Hugly), Malla and Magadha. The Mārkaṇḍeya P., 57, 44, in an almost identical verse, substitutes for Muṇḍa the name of Madra, which is evidently erroneous, because the Madras are in the Punjab. It can be seen here, by yet another example, how very unstable proper names are unless their fame is sufficient to ensure their preservation. Further on, we do not hesitate to recognise the Muṇḍa in the Maṇḍika which the Mahā Bhārata, Calcutta edition, III, 253, 15243, classes among the peoples conquered by Karṇa in his campaign in eastern India, along with Aṅga, Vaṅga, Kaliṅga, in the one case and Mithila, Magadha, Karkakhaṇḍa in the other. The surroundings very exactly define the Muṇḍa. The Bombay text reads Śuṇḍika, an ethnic otherwise unknown. The southern recension in the corresponding passage III, 255, 8, has the same reading Śuṇḍika, but the editors record from two other manuscripts the reading Muṇḍika, which would be simply a secondary form of Muṇḍa.

5. *Pulinda-Kulinda.*—The name of the Pulindas is known throughout Sanskrit literature. The Aitareya Brāhmaṇa, 7, 18, classes them among the *udantya* "outside the [Aryan] limits," with the Andhra, the Puṇḍra, the Sabara, the Mūtiba, attached to the clan of Viśvāmitra, but essentially formed of *dasyu* "savages." They are found along with the Andhra in the XIIIth edict of Aśoka, amidst the peoples who are established on the military frontier of the empire, but follow the law proclaimed by the Emperor. Buddhism classes them among the 'inferior races' (*nīcakula*), the "barbarians" (*mleccha*), the "frontier populations" (*pratyanta janapada*) with the Caṇḍāla, Mātaṅga, Śabara, Pukkasa, Domba (Mahāvyutpatti, 188, 15). The Mahāvaṁśa, 7, 68 connects their origin with the children born of the union of Vijaya, the conqueror of Ceylon, with the Yakkha princess Kuvaṇṇā. In the Jaina literature they appear in the canonical list of the Mlecchas (*Ind. St.*, 16, 352, *Praśnavyākaraṇa* ; 397, *Prajñāpanā*) and their women in the conventional list of royal slaves (*ibid*, 313, 380, 412). The Rāmāyana, 4, 43, 11 B ; 44, 12 G, locates them in the

north of India between the Matsya (Mleccha B.) and the Śūrasena that is to say between Alvar and Mathura. The Mahā Bhārata also considers them Mleccha; it is they who are to reign on the earth in the Kali age, with the Andhra, the Śaka, the Yavana and the Kamboja, III, 188, 12839; they are met with again in the same company, XIII, 33, 2104, among the races fallen to the rank of Śūdra (*Vṛṣala*) because they did not see Brāhmans. They appear frequently in the great epic, but always in bad company: Pauṇḍra, Yavana, Kirāta, Cīna and other Mlecchas, 1, 175, 6685; Dravida, Andhra, and other Mlecchas, V, 160, 5510; Daśārṇa, Mekala, Utkala, VI, 9, 347. The condition of sinners in hell is like that of the Pulinda, XII, 151, 5620; the sinners will be reborn in the south in the families of Andhra, Pulinda, Sabara, XII, 207, 7559. The Pulinda derive their origin from the foam thrown off by the cow of Vasiṣṭha, I, 175, 6685. Bhīma, the conqueror of the east, turns towards the south, finds them on his way when marching on Cedi, II, 29, 1068, and reduces their city (*nagara*). Sahadeva, who has just reduced eastern Kosala, meets with them, II, 31, 1120 before fighting with Pāṇḍya, Kiṣkindhyā, and Māhiṣmatī. In the legend of Udayana, elaborated by the author of the Bṛhatkathā, the Pulindas are the allies and the auxiliaries of the king of Kauśāmbi, during his love-affair with Vāsavadattā (*Kathā S. Sāg.*, II, 12). Their kingdom is situated amidst the Vindhyas, on the route which goes from Kauśāmbi to Ujjayinī. Their king adores the cruel Devī, offers her human victims, and pillages the caravans (*ibid*, IV, 22). The Bṛhatkathā-ślokasaṁgraha, always impregnated with a picturesque realism, which it certainly owes to its model, draws a striking picture of the Pulinda, VIII, 31; a group of young men leave for the chase; one of them tells the party: "I see before us an innumerable army of these Pulindas who haunt the caverns of the forest, appearing like a forest of trunks blackened in the fire. From their ranks come a fat little man small as a dwarf, and with copper-coloured eyes: it was their chief Siṁhaśatru ('Enemy of the lions'). He saluted the commander-in-chief who asked him: 'How is the wife of my brother? And your two sons, Śāmbara (deer) and Sāraṅga (antilope)—are they in good health?' Rumaṅvat ordered to hand over to Siṁhaśatru a bale of stuffs dyed with indigo, curcuma, and safran, besides a thousand jars of sesamum oil......Then appeared before us deer whose limbs flashed fire like diamond bubbles; in bands, they passed and repassed, as swift as the wind. ......One asks the chief of the Pulindas: 'None of us has ever seen such beasts! If you know about them, explain them to us!' 'Neither do I know about them,' said the Pulinda, 'but my father did. On a certain occasion, he taught me something which I will tell you. ...He whose arrow, once let fly, makes a pradakṣiṇa around these beasts to return forthwith to the quiver, know that he is a cakravartin' (transl. Lacote, 55). All the traits here appear life-like. The Pulindas are compared to the burnt trunks; the Nāṭyaśāstra, XXI, 89, in fact, prescribes that the Pulinda should be represented with a black complexion. The chief is of the size of a dwarf (*nikharva*): "The Pre-Dravidians......differentiate themselves from the Dravidians by their short stature" (Thurston, *The Madras Presidency*, p. 124). The sons of the chief have the names of animals; totemism is still spread amongst the savage tribes of the plateaus. The history of the arrows which return to the quiver and the resplendent deer appear to come directly from the folklore of the Mundas the Santals.

The name of the Pulindas is interpreted in Tibetan (Mahāvyut., 188, 15) by *gyuṅ po* "out-cast" and in Chinese by *tu-kia* [1] "the race which kills the beasts for their food." Ptolemy, VII, 1, 64, also gives to the Poulindai the epithet of *agriophagoi*, a rare term, which appears to be invented to translate an Indian original; *agrio°* signifies "wild," *°phagos* "eater of......;" one hesitates to make a choice between "who live on wild fruits" and "who live on raw meat." He assigns to them a well-defined place in the interior behind Larikē, the country of the Lāṭa, which has for its principal towns amongst others; Barygaza (Bharukaccha), Ozēne (Ujjayinī) and Nasika (Nāsika), from Malva to the source of the Godāvarī. It is therefore in the hills of Satpura, the Vindhya, and the Aravalli that they are located by him. Still further away, in the interior, he says, are the Khatriaoi of whom the cities are, partly to the east and partly to the west of the Indus.

The Kulindas have not acquired the same celebrity as the Pulindas. Their name is rarely met with after the epic period. In the Mahā Bhārata, however, their rôle is more considerable than that of the Pulindas. They live "amidst the Himālaya in a country which abounds in elephants and in horses, all mixed with the Kirāta, the Taṅgaṇa and also with the Pulinda (*sic*) in hundreds, a country loved by the gods, full of innumerable marvels, III, 140, 10866; their king Subāhu receives with respect the Pāṇḍavas when they set out to visit the Gandhamādana; when returning, they follow the same way, pass through Cīna, Tukhāra, Darada "and then they found the countries of the Kulinda that have so many jewels, and after crossing the Himalayan region there where walking is difficult, they saw the fortress of the king Subāhu" III, 177, 12350. Arjuna setting out to subdue the north begins with the conquest of the Kulinda; then he turns towards Ānarta, Kālakūṭa, Śakala, II, 26, 996. In the Rājasūya of Yudhiṣṭhira, the Kulinda appear in the cortège of the northern peoples, inhabitants of the banks of the river Sailodā: Khasa, Pārada, Taṅgaṇa, etc., which bring as tribute the gold of ant-hills, the chowries made of the tails of yaks and the honey of the mountain, II, 52, 1859. Section 85 of the VIII book relates at length the struggle in which the Kulindas were engaged, during the great battle, mounted on their swift elephants, well-equipped, covered with gold and born in the Himālaya. In the description of the world, VI, 9, 370, the Kulindas are classed near the Pārada and the Kuṇṭhaka; the country has its Piémont, the Kulindopatyaka, VI, 9, 363. But once again here, as we have already observed in other cases, the surreptitious variants attest that the name is not understood; the name of Kaliṅga, which is better known, tends to supplant it; VI, 9, 347 C has *Kaliṅga*; VII, 121, 4819 C has *Kuliṅga* and the translator of P. C. Roy writes *Kaliṅga*. The Vāyu P. 45, 116 writes Kulinda in the list of the *Udīcya* "Northerners": *Gāndhārā Yavanāś caiva*, etc., the Matsya P., in the corresponding verse 113, 41 substitutes *Pulinda* which is better known, but wrongly placed here; the Mārkaṇḍeya, 57, 37 substitutes *Kaliṅga*. We recall these mentions of Kuliṅga which we have already seen alternating through confusion with the Bhuliṅga. Another variant is worthy of notice. The Mahā Bhārata, XIII, 33, 2104, in the list of degraded tribes, already quoted, writes: *Kalindāś ca Pulindāś ca*; P. C. Roy's translator introduces here the Kaliṅga. But the sketch of Indian geography given by Vāgbhaṭa (*Kāvyānuśāsanaṁ°*) and copied by Hemacandra (*Kāvyānuśāsana*, 12‹), enumerating the northern mountains, beyond Pṛthūdaka (Pehoa), gives: *Himālaya-Jālandhara-Kalind-Endrakīla*............. *parvatāḥ*; Hemacandra writes "*Kalindrendra*." probably under the influence of the following syllable *dra*. It is interesting to state that the form collected by Ptolemy VII, 1, 42 *Kulindri(nē)*, presents the same alteration; the analogy of the name of Indra, so popular and so frequently used at the end of compounds, has not failed to affect the final °*inda*. As regards the vowel of the initial syllable, the *a* can be original, as in Kaliṅga; the hypothesis is rendered probable by the sacred name of the holy Yamuna. This is *Kālindī* (Amara, I, 10, 31) "the daughter of the mountain Kalinda," as the Narmadā is "the daughter of the mountain Mekala" (Amara, *ibid*, the same verse). Ptolemy VII, 1, 42 places the Kulindrinē "below the sources of the Bibasis (Vipāśā), the Zaradros (Śatadru), the Diamouna (Yamunā) and the Ganges." The Yamunā is therefore exactly the daughter of the mountains of the Kulinda country. The Greek geography confirms the Indian evidences.

The Bṛhatsaṁhitā of Varāha Mihira supplies another variant of the same name. In the XIV chapter, the editor H. Kern has twice adopted the reading *Kauṇinda*, in preference to other readings *Kaulinda* and *Kaulindra* furnished by equally good manuscripts. Undoubtedly it refers to the Kulinda; in verse 30, they appear in a catalogue of the peoples of the North-East, with Kirāta and Cīna, two lines after Abhisāra-Darada-Taṅgaṇa-Kulūta; in verse 33, the King Kauṇinda follows Āvanta, Ānarta, Sindhu-Sauvira, Hārahaura and the sovereign of Madra. In the same treatise, but in another chapter, IV, 24, the printed text has Kaulinda, with the variant *Kaulindra*, in a list which includes Traigarta, Mālava, Sibi, Āyodhyaka. The form *Kuṇinda* is warranted, in any case, by the legend of a large number of old coins, found mostly in the districts of Saharanpur and Ambala "the Piémont of the Kulinda." These pieces are either silver or copper; the work is quite varied, and they cover, certainly, a fairly long period of time, beginning from the second century before the Christian era. The design is overloaded; on the obverse a woman standing with her left hand in her hip, offering with her right hand a fruit to a stag (or a buffalo) standing and turned to its right, bearing a symbol between its horns; over its chine, a kind of square railing crowned by a parasol; on the reverse a caitya with three stories of arches surmounted by the parasol; on the right, a tree inside a railing; on the left, a Svastika and a symbol with triangular head; higher up, a nandipada; below, a serpent. The legend is most often written in two scripts, Brāhmi and Kharoṣṭrī; in Brāhmī: *Amagābhutisa Maharajasa rañaḥ* (*rājña*) *Kuṇadasa*; the Kharoṣṭrī: *Raña Kuṇidasa Amaghabhatisā Maharajasa*. The use of the two writings, each of which characterises a world and a civilisation, indicates well the importance of the region occupied by the Kulinda-Kuṇinda; it is also in their territory, or very near them, in the valley of Kangra, that digraphic inscriptions in Brāhmī and Kharoṣṭhī have been discovered (*Ep. Ind.*, *VII*, 116).

Pulinda-Kulinda, Mekala-Utkala (with the group Uḍra-Puṇḍra-Muṇḍa), Kosala-Tosala, Aṅga-Vaṅga, Kaliṅga-Tiliṅga form the links of a long chain which extends from the eastern confines of Kashmir up to the centre of the peninsula. The skeleton of this ethnical system is constituted by the heights of the central plateau; it participates in the life of all the great rivers of India, except the Indus in the west and the Kaveri in the south. Each of these groups form a binary whole; each of these binary units is united with another member of the system. In each ethnic pair the twin bears the same name, differentiated only by the initial: *k* and *t*; *k* and *p*; zero and *v*, or *m* or *p*. This process of formation is foreign to Indo-European; it is foreign to Dravidian; it is on the contrary characteristic of the vast family of languages which are called Austro-Asiatic, and which covers in India the group of the Muṇḍā languages, often called also the Kolarian. Dr. Sten Konow, who has made a special study of these languages, *Linguistic Survey of India*, Vol. IV; *Muṇḍā* and *Dravidian Languages*; writes (introd., p. 9): "The principal abode of the Muṇḍā languages is at present in the plateau of Chota Nagpur; they are spoken also in the districts of Madras and the Central Provinces which are neighbouring to them, and in the Mahadeo hills. For nearly all cases they are found in the jungles and on the hills, the plains and the valleys being inhabited by an Aryan-speaking population....The Muṇḍā languages must have been formerly spoken over a vast area in Central India and probably also in the valley of the Ganges." Father Schmidt in his study on *Les peuples Mon-khmér, trait-d'union entre les peuples de l'Asie Centrale et de l'Austronésie* (trad. franc., B. É. F. E. O., VII), compares the Muṇḍā languages with the Mōn-Khmêr languages, and notes that the "system of formation of words with the help of prefixes and suffixes is identical in both :

"*a.* In these two groups of languages, all the consonants that these languages possess, with the exception of *ṅ*, *n'*, *y* and *w*, can serve as simple prefixes, and, as in most of the Mōn-Khmêr languages, one obtains in the Muṇḍā languages also a second degree of prefixation by the insertion of a nasal *ṅ*, *n'*, *m*, *n*, or a liquid *r* [*l* ?], between the prefix and the root.

"*b.* The infix *n* forms in the Mōn-Khmêr languages especially the names of instruments, in the Muṇḍā languages abstract names, which designate the result of an action ; but the forms of this last kind are not rare either particularly in Khmêr, Bahnar and Nicobarese."

The names which we have studied present formations which correspond well with the general type described by Father Schmidt. One cannot help being struck by the analogies which bring them together. Three series : Pulinda-Kulinda, Aṅga-Vaṅga, Kaliṅga-Triliṅga have a nasal in the interior which can be an infix ; the secondary series, Uḍra-Puṇḍra-Muṇḍa, appears to show the fluctuation of the infix, attested also by the sporadic variants Uṇḍa, Oṇḍa, Oṇḍra = Uḍra. One is tempted to ask whether the synonymous designations Utkala and Uḍra, are not in reality the same word, differentiated by the presence or the absence of an infix *k*. One would have *Ut* (*ka*) *la* = *Uḍ-ra* ; the difference of the dental in one case and of the cerebral in another, cannot create any difficulty ; in the presence of the guttural surd, the explosive is more easily dental ; combined with *r*, the cerebral is preserved, all the more so because it is a question of rendering foreign sounds in Sanskrit and in that case writing has a tendency to use the less usual sounds and characters. If the connection of Utkala-Uḍra is admissible, one will be naturally brought to connect Mekal-Muṇḍa (-Mundra, Muṇḍra). Two series: Kosala-Tosala, Utkala-Mekala have the same final.

By prosecuting a systematic research, one will find, we are sure, other groups constituted after the same type; we will point out here only the group Accha-Vaccha, exactly symmetrical with Aṅga-Vaṅga; we have not included it in our list as it lacks sufficient precision; we have retained only the ethnics that are precisely localised, where the proximity accompanies the verbal resemblance, in order to eliminate as much as possible the risks of a purely accidental homophony. Accha-Vaccha are named side by side in the Jaina texts, *e.g.*, Bhagavatī, 15, 17, a list of the native peoples opposed to the "barbarians": Aṅga, Vaṅga, Magaha, Malaya, Mālavya, Accha, Vaccha, Koccha, etc. (*Ind. Stud.*, 16, 304), and Prajñāpanā, a list of the Āriya peoples, 3rd verse: *Vairāḍa Vattha* (°*ccha B*) *Varaṇā Atthā* (°*cchā* B C) (*ibid*, 398). The commentator explains *Vatseṣu Vairāṭapuram*; but, as Weber remarks, the Vatsa have already been mentioned in the preceding verse with the city of Kosambi (Kauśāmbi) which is in fact their capital. Nemicandra, in his commentary, substitutes Maccha=Matsya and Vairāta is in fact the capital of the Matsya country. But Accha is unknown; the commentator admits the confusion and the ignorance of the interpreters: *Varuṇo* (sic) *nagaram Acchā deśāh anye tu Varuṇe Acchā purīty āhuḥ.*

We have left aside for identical reasons, the names of cities which offer an alternance of the same kind. We had occasion to study, in a previous paper the alternance of Takkola-Kakkola as the name of a city and as the name of a plant. We had not then to search for the starting point of this alternance. Now we can see that it brings us back to the play of the Austro-Asiatic preformatives. The Lepcha dictionary of Mainwaring and Grünwedel gives, p. 10, *Kak-lo* "cardamoms, Amomum," and p. 116 *ta-kól* "a kind of fern, *Asplenium esculentum*," *t.-k.-bí* "the same as vegetable." We have left aside also the names of vegetables which merit a special study; we will point out here as a specimen of possible researches only synonymous words of *kṣumā* and *umā* "the flax" which are related to the difficult problem of the history of flax and which sound so strangely like the Chinese designation *hu-ma* [1] always interpreted, on the strength of the characters, as "the Iranian (*hu*) hemp (*ma*)"; but Japanese has, for *Linum usitatissimum*, *a-ma* [2] where Iran has nothing to do and beside the character for hemp [3] which is read *ma* in Chinese, is read as *asa* in Japanese. It is significant that the derivatives of the two Sanskrit forms fall under two categories: *kṣauma*, from *kṣumā*, applies only to the tissue of flax, to the wrought flax; *aumīna* and *umya* (Pāṇ., 5, 2, 4, and Pat., *ad. loc.*; Amara, 2, 9, 7; Hemacandra, 967) apply only to the field in which the plant is cultivated. The history of the goddess Umā-Pārvatī should be reconsidered from this point of view. We can still observe that though *kṣauma* and its congeners have subsisted up to the present time, *umā* and its derivatives have altogether disappeared after Pāṇini, being replaced by the word *atasī* and its derivatives. Perhaps the ancient name of the plant, sanctified

[1] 胡麻 [2] 亞麻 [3] 麻

by religion, might have been forbidden; it might have become taboo.

We have seen already that "as in most of the Mon-Khmêr languages, so also in the Muṇḍā languages a second degree of prefixation is obtained by the insertion of a nasal or of a liquid between the prefix and the root." One is therefore brought to suppose that amongst the geographical names of India, those which begin by *kam, kar, kal, tam, tar, tal, pam, par, pal* can occasionally preserve the indications of the Austro-Asiatic past. Here the research is more delicate, the results are more doubtful; we have not succeeded in finding out organic wholes of this type that are inseparable like those we have already examined. It is possible that *Kaliṅga, Tiliṅga* may belong to this type and may be analysed as *kal-i(ṅ)ga, til-i(ṅ)ga*. The variation of the first vowel can be easily explained by the hypothesis of a vowel of obscure timbre ə, which is wanting in the Aryan languages of India, and which could have taken the most diverse shades. The name of Kaliṅga has been fixed under this form at an early time because Kaliṅga played an important role in the political history of India as soon as the Aryan civilisation had spread up to the eastern coast: witness the inscriptions of Aśoka and Khāravela. Tiliṅga has not the same fortune; the Aryan and Dravidian conquest had cut it into pieces; the variations of its name indicate its political variations; it is only about the year 1000 A.D. that some princes claimed "the suzerainty of Trikaliṅga," perhaps with the intention of absorbing both T(r)iliṅga and Kaliṅga under this designation. It is equally possible that *Kulinda-Pulinda* originated from *Kəl-inda, Pəl-inda*; we have met with *Kalinda*, *Kālindī* and on the other hand we have seen, more than once, the variant *Kuliṅga* instead of *Kalinga* and the ethnique *Bhuliṅga* has also an *u*. Experts in the Austro-Asiatic languages may venture, risky as it often is in matters of local onomastic, to propose etymologies for these names. Father Schmidt, without thinking of it, has already suggested for *Kaliṅga* an etymology which, if correct, would open a direction for new researches. In the list of lexicographic correspondences accompanying his article B. E. F. E. O., VII, 261, he writes under the rubric of words with initial L (n. 151) : "*Kalāṅ* [in Nicobarese], white-bellied sea-eagle, *Cuncuma lemogaster*=Khmêr *Khleṅ*, Stieng *Kliṅ*, a kind of milan (Sanskrit *Kaliṅga*) : The Sanskrit Kaliṅga can very well signify 'the shrike with a forked tail,' Am. 2, 5, 16 ; Hem.; 1333. Böhtlingk and Roth suggest (P. W.[1], sub verbo) for this meaning, an analysis of the word into *Kaliṁ+ga* ; they had been, without knowing it, anticipated by Sarvānanda, who comments, on Am., 2, 5, 16 : *kaliṁ gahanaṁ gacchatīti Kaliṅgaḥ*. Kṣīrasvāmin, has also his own interpretation : *ke liṅgaṁ cūḍāsya kaliṅgaḥ* 'it has on its head (*ka*) its characteristic sign, its tuft.'" These fancies are a useful reminder of the shifting ground of etymology. If the correspondence indicated by Father Schmidt be recognised as exact, one would be led to suppose that the eponyms of regions that we have studied were totems. But the word *Kaliṅga* cannot fail to suggest a completely different connection with the Tibetan word *gliṅ*=Sk. *dvipa*. Tibetan, of course, belongs neither to the Muṇḍā family nor to the Austro-Asiatic group; but it has so many features in common with these languages that it cannot be completely kept aside from them. The word *gliṅ*, now-a-days pronounced *liṅ* in the classical use of Lhasa, contains a prefix *g*=*ka*;

Tibetan has transformed into sonants all the surd explosives of the preformatives: *g*, *d*, *b*, for *k* (*a*), *t* (*a*), *p* (*a*), and eliminated the vocalic element which sustained them. The word *gliṅ* fall back therefore on an older form *ka-liṅ*. Its meaning is identical to Sanskrit *dvīpa* "island," with all the secondary meanings deriving from it: "Isolated territory, territorial division large or small," etc. The simple word, without a preformative, can be met with in Sikkim, amongst the Lepchas who are considered to be the most ancient inhabitants of the country; it is *lyaṅ* "the earth" in every sense of the word: "the earth, territory," etc. In Tibetan, the word *g-liṅ* is combined with the affix *-ka*; *g-liṅ-ka* means, according to S. C. Das, "garden"; "pleasure park"; the English-Tibetan dictionary of Lama Dawasamdup Kazi renders, in fact, the English word *garden* by *ldum-ra*; *gliṅ-ka*; *chod z'iṅ*. Jäschke, however, gives for *gliṅ-ka* "a small uncultivated river-island or low land." In Lepcha, too, the word *lyaṅ* is combined with the affix *-ka* to designate "a space where there is no village." It seems impossible to isolate this word from the name of *Laṅkā*, which designates in Sanskrit the island *par excellence*, the island of the Rākṣasas, where reigns the demon Rāvaṇa, the violent adversary of divine Rāma. The vocabulary of Yule and Burnell, *Hobson-Jobson*, *s. v. Lunka* adds "also an island in general." The learned compilers have probably borrowed this indication from the Telugu Dictionary of Brown. They indicate still another meaning of the word. "A kind of strong cheroot much prized in the Madras Presidency and so called from being made of tobacco grown in the 'islands' (the local term of which is *laṅka*) of the Godavery delta." No reference at all; it is therefore from the real usage that they have gathered this signification, which we had not the occasion to verify on the place. The *laṅka* cigar brings us back in an unexpected manner to Kaliṅga with the islands of the Godavari delta. And in fact the *Gazetter of India*,[1] s. v. *Godavari*, fully confirms this evidence: "The land on which tobacco is grown consists for the most part of alluvial islands lying within the banks of the Godavari river, called *lankás*, which are flooded every year......... Tobacco seems to be grown on any part of the *lankás* almost indifferently......... The tobacco of the *lankás* would command a good price in European markets." The word is therefore a current one. But some epigraphic documents prove that this vocable was equally in use more in the north, in the valley of the Mahanadi. A deed of gift, which comes from the state of Sonpur on the Mahanadi and published by B. C. Mazumdar (Ep. Ind., XII, 237), is issued by a local prince related by an unknown *lien* with the sovereign of Trikaliṅga, and which takes title of *Paścimalaṅkādhi-pati*; Mr. Mazumdar observes about this name that "the peoples of Sonpur still know by tradition that the state of Sonpur once bore some name as *Paścimalaṅkā*." Another document coming from the same state and published by the same editor (Ep. Ind., XII, 218) is granted *Laṅkāvarttakasaṁnidhau*. The editor proposes to identify Laṅkāvarttaka with a high land to be found in the bed of the Mahanadi and which is called Laṅkeś-varī. The two inscriptions are of very late epoch and go back only three or four centuries earlier. One cannot read in Pliny without surprise, the passage already cited, VI, 18: *Insula in Gange est magnæ amplitudinis gentem continens unam nomine Modogalingam.* "There is an island of large extent in the Ganges, which contains only one nation called Modogalinga." Whatever may be the first element (*cf. ante*) the mention of the island in the Ganges recalls inevitably *glin* (=*ga-ling*) which signifies island and these *laṅkā* which we find in the bed of the Godavari and the Mahanadi up the Ganges.

The element *laṅkā* reappears in a certain number of geographical names in the neighbourhood of the Malaya peninsula. One can have no hesitation in recognising it in the country of *Kia-mo-lang-kia*, *Lang-kia*, *Lang-kia shu*, of the Chinese travellers and annalists, *Leṅkasuku* of Nāgarakrĕtāgama, *Ilaṅgaśogam* of the Tamil inscription of Rājendracola I in Tanjore. Mr. Ferrand has collected all the texts in an Appendix (III) of his article on Malaka (*J. A.*, 1918, II, 134, 145, and 153); he has discussed there the proposed localisations and has located it with much probability on the eastern coast of the Malaya peninsula, right in the Isthmus of Ligor. The identity *Kia-mo-lang-kia* = *Lang-kia-shu*, generally admitted, supposes that the word *laṅka* forms an organic element in the whole name; besides, Yi-tsing does not hesitate to use alternatively, in course of the same passage, *Lang-kia-shu* and *Lang-kia* (*Relig. Émin.*, p. 57 and 100); the History of the Leang dynasty also gives the two forms *Lang-ya* and *Lang-ya-sieou*. The meaning of the final element; *su*, *śuk*, *śoga* remains to be determined. As regards the word *Kia-mo-lang-kia*, by which Hiuan-tsang designates the same country (*Mém.*, II, 82), Stanislas Julien has constituted the Sanskrit original *Kāmalaṅkā* on the basis of the type of *Kāmarūpa* in which also the first two syllables are equally represented by the characters *kia-mo* [1]

[1] 迦 麻

and this restitution has been accepted without discussion. However Mr. Ferrand (J. A., 1918. II, 145), who is familiar with the Malayan languages, has presented a sagacious observation of this name. "*Kāmalaṅkā*," he says, "is a curious form of toponomastic. One cannot help connecting the first two syllables with those of the Sanskrit name of Assam, Kāmarūpa. It cannot be doubted that in both cases the Sanskrit *kāma* 'love' is simply a pun recalling by assonance, more or less exactly, the indigenous word." Judging by the native terms used in Hiuan-tsang's transcription, it is probable that his Indian informants had pronounced *Kāmalaṅka.* But this name had certainly taken still another form in Sanskrit, in the time of Hiuan-tsang. The Mañjuśrīmūlakalpa, the Sanskrit original of which has been discovered by the admirable Gaṇapati Śāstrī, and of which we have also a Tibetan and an incomplete Chinese translation, names the islands of Karmaraṅga with the island of cocoanuts and Vāruṣaka (Baros, Sumatra) and the islands of the naked (Nicobar), Bali and Java as the regions where the language is indistinct, without clearness, rude, and abounding in the letter *r*.

*Karmaraṅgākhyadvīpeṣu Nāḍikerasamudbhave* | *dvīpe Vāruṣake caiva Nagna Balisamudbhave* | *Yavadvīpe vā sattveṣu tadanyadvīpasamudbhavā* | *Vācā rakārabahulā tu vācā asphuṭatāṁ gatā* | *avyaktā niṣṭurā caiva sakrodhapretayoniṣu.*

Ed. Gaṇapati; II p. 322.

I shall not stop to consider here all the names which are so important for the study of Indian archipelago; I have already made them the subject of a communication to the Société Asiatique (J. A., 1921, I, 332) and which I propose to publish later on. The Chinese translation omits in this passage the name of Karmaraṅga. The Tibetan translation (ed. of Pekin, p. 197a) gives as its equivalent *las chon*= "action-colour;" it is the literal translation of the two words *karma* (action) and *raṅga* (colour), which had been believed to be discovered on the analysis of the name of the country. The form of the word Karmaraṅga, with its two *r*, attests the frequency of the sound *r* in this group of languages. The sound *r* has been substituted for the *l* of *laṇkà* and also been introduced in the first element. The word, however, is not absolutely isolated. Bāṇa, in the Harṣacarita, twice mentions the shields of Karmaraṅga in the course of the seventh chapter (edit. Nirnayasagar, p. 232); the warriors who surrounded Harṣa wore as ornaments the leathern bucklers of Karmaraṅga which were round and variegated (*kirmīra-kārmaraṅgacarmamaṇḍalamaṇḍan*°; *ibid*, p. 243); among the presents sent by the king of Kāmarūpa, there were the leathern bucklers of Karmaraṅga ornamented with designs drawn by the lustre of gold and with beautiful borders: *rucirakāñcanapattrabhaṅgabhaṅgurāṇām atibandhuraparivesānām Kārmaraṅgacarmaṇām sambhārān*. The Kashmir edition has the reading *kārmaraṅga*; the Bombay texts followed by Cowell in his translation, pp. 203 and 214, read *kārdaraṅga*; the epithet *kirmīra* intentionally selected for the alliteration, would suffice to warrant the reading *kārmaraṅga*, made still more suitable by the use of the word *carma* which follows it: *kirmīrakārmaraṅgacarma*. The commentator Śaṁkara, in his Saṁketa comments on the first passage: *kārdaraṅgakāni kārdaraṅgadeśodbhavāni bahusuvarṇasūtraracitāni carmāṇi. sphoṭakāḥ snigdhavarṇamāṁsasphārāṇi kārdaraṅgacarmāṇi*: "the leather coming from the country of Kārdaraṅga, fabricated with many golden threads; the skins of Kārdaraṅga have a lump of flesh of glistening colour," on the second passage he repeats that Kārdaraṅga is the name of the country of origin of these bucklers: *Kārdaraṅgadeśabhavānāṁ spheṭakānām*. It is therefore necessary to reject the explanation given by Böhtlingk (*P W*², *sub verbo*): "*hochroth* (bright red); cf. *kṛmirāga*." Besides Karmaraṅga, the Mañjuśrimūlakalpa mentions also the name of Carmaraṅga twice in chap. 20, p. 206, and in chap. 22, p. 233; in both the passages Carmaraṅga is mentioned along with Kalaśavarapura (Kalaśāhvā, p. 206; Kalaśamukhya, p. 233) Samataṭa and Vaṅga. The last two countries lead us to the delta of the Ganges; Kalaśapura (or Kalaśavarapura, etc.) is a city of Suvarṇadvīpa according to the evidence of the Kathāsaritsāgara, 54, 108 (the Mañjarī, in the corresponding tale, XV, 207 ff., does not give the name of the city). In the collection of Nepalese miniatures studied by M. Foucher (*Étude sur l'Iconographie bouddhique de l'Inde*), the representation of "Bhagavat at Kalaśavarapura" (MS. A. 15, Calcutta, n° 13) immediately follows that of "Dīpaṅkara in Yavadvīpa" (*ibid*; n. 12). M. Pelliot has collected (B. E. F. E.-O, IV, 360) several Chinese texts which mention this city and from which it is evident that Kalaśapura was situated in the north of To-ho-lo, itself located in the north of Pan-pan which lies on the Malaya peninsula, in the same line as Bandon or Ligor. Carmaraṅga therefore brings us to the same regions as Karmaraṅga and is perhaps only a variant of the same name. It should be observed that the two chapters of Mañjuśrīmūlakalpa in which the name of Carmaraṅga is met with are wanting not only in the Chinese version but also in the Tibetan version of the work. The Bṛhatsaṁhitā, XIV, 9, in its catalogue of the peoples of the South-East (*āgneyī*) combines *Vṛṣa-Nālikera-Carmadvīpaḥ*; Kern has translated (*J. R. A. S.*, n. s., V, 83) this as "The Island of Bulls, of Cocoas, of Tree-barks," but the mention of *Nālikera* by the side of *carma* clearly proves that Carmadvīpa corresponds here to Carma- or Karma-raṅgadvīpa of the Mañjuśrīmūlakalpa. The Bṛhatsaṁhitā, in the same chapter, verse 23, mentions a people of Carmaraṅga again amongst the populations of the farthest North-West, pêle-mêle with the Śulika (Sogdians), the Ekavilocana (Monophthalmes), Dīrghagrīva (long-necked), etc. This refers, without doubt, to the same people that the Mahā Bhārata, VI, 9, 355 calls Carmamaṇḍala and the Purāṇas (Mārk., 57, 36; Vāy., 45, 115) call Carmakhaṇḍika. Mr. Pargiter has connected this last denomination with the name of Samarcand. In fact they are enumerated between the Pahlava and the Gāndhāra, and thus would be located on the confines of the Indian and Iranian world.

The reputation of the skins of Karmaraṅga appears to explain Ptolemy's note on the population of the "Brigands" λῃσταί which he locates exactly in the surroundings of Karmaraṅga, on the southern shores of the great gulf, *i.e.*, the Gulf of Siam (VII, 2, 6 and 21): "It is said that the natives of the country of Brigands live like beasts, inhabit the caverns, and that they have skin almost like that of hippopotami impenetrable by arrows." The region had some centres of population and even a port of commerce: "Samara(n)dē, Pagrasa, Pithōnobastē which is a market, Akadra, Zabai which is the city." It can be supposed that Samara(n)dē is an alteration of the name which has finally taken in Sanskrit the alternate forms Carmaraṅga and Karmaraṅga (*cf. infra* the forms *Camariz, Camarix*).

India received not only some bucklers of Karmaraṅga hide; she also received from this country a fruit which has been acclimatized in India and which continues to bear even to-day, but slightly transformed, the name of its land of origin. *Karmaraṅga* is the Sanskrit designation of the fruit which the Europeans call *carambole*; Lushington (*List of Vernacular Trees...in the Madras Presidency*, n° 365) mentions also the names of the Coromandel Gooseberry; Sweet Climbing; Square Tamarind. According to the same authority the Uriya name is *koromoṅga* (by metathesis), in Telugu *koromoṅga* and *tamarta*, in Tamil *śagadam, śiśam, śīgam, kandaśaḍgam, tamarattāi*; in Malayalam *śaturappuḷi, kāmaran'gam, puliññi, tamaratta*, in Canarese *dārehuḷi, karmaraṅga, kirinelli, dārepuḷi*; Khory and Katrak (*Materia Medica*, II, 152) adds for Bengali *kamaraṅga* and *kamarak*, for Gujrati *kamarak*, for Hindi *kamaraṅga* and *kamrakh*. According to the Hindi Śabda Sāgara, *kamarakh* is the name of the tree; the name of the fruit is (in Hindi) *kamaraṅga* and *karmaraṅga*. Thus in the designation of this fruit we find again the fluctuation attested by *Kamaraṅga* (Kia-mo-lang-kia) of Hiuan-tsang against *Karmaraṅga* of the Mañjuśrīmūlakalpa. The glossary of Yule and Burnell has an excellent and copious article on this fruit, s.v. *carambola*. The name has been registered by Linné who has classified the tree under the title of *Averrhoa Carambola*. The original habitat of the tree is the islands of Moluccas (Lushington, *loc. cit.*); the Karmaraṅga in this case cou. represent a stage in the transplantation of the carambol tree; this country, therefore, would from very early times, have been a market of exchange between India and the farthest islands of the archipelago.[1] Its situation on the eastern coast of the isthmus of Ligor marked it out for this role. The Chinese texts collected by M. Ferrand confirm the fact ; the most expressive of these texts appear to me to be the biography of Paramārtha translated by Takakusu (B.E.F.E.O., IV. 62). When the Indian monk, tired of his sojourn in China, wished to return to his country (he was a native of Ujjayinī), his biographer only says : "he thought of embarking for *Lang-kia-su.*"

The name of Karmaraṅga is mentioned in the famous inscription of Rājendracola I at Tanjore although no one has yet recognised it. In the list of countries conquered by the Indian conqueror, after Ilaṅgaśogam come Māpappāḷam, Mevilimbaṅgam, Vaḷaippandūṟu, Taḷaittakkolam, Mādamāliṅgam. I have already dealt with Taḷaittakkolam elsewhere in connection of Takkola of Ptolemy and the Pali texts ; I shall have to return to the last name directly. "Mevilimbaṅgam and Vaḷaippandūṟu do not afford any identification at present," says M. Coedès

1 The name of *carmaraṅga* is given by Rājanighaṇṭu, 3, 123 as a synonymn of *āvartikā* which is the name for the senna *Cassia acutifolia* (Lushington, *List*, 955 : African senna, *Kordofan s.*, *Nubian s.*, *Officinal s.*, *Senaar s.*, *Surat s.*). As these designations indicate, the plant is a native of Nubia and Abyssinia. The name *Carmaraṅga* does not appear to point to the place of origin. This name has not yet been met with in either learned or ordinary usage except for the reference made by the Rājanighaṇṭu compiled at a very late period, probably in the thirteenth century. Among other names of senna collected in this compilation appears also *ran'galatā* in which *raṅga* is not accompanied by *carma*. Lushington's list does not mention any of these names for *Cassia acutifolia*.

in his fine article on the kingdom of Śrīvijaya (*B. E. F. E. O.*, XVIII, 6, 15). M. Ferrand has only reproduced the name without adding anything to it in his detailed review of this work (*J. A.*, 1919, II, 172). The Malaya name of the carambol tree is *balimbing* or *belimbing*; in India this name is used for a variety of carambol tree, the *Averrhoa Bilimbi* of Linné, which yields a sweeter fruit than karmaraṅga; in Telugu: *bilibili*, *bilumbi*, *gommarēku*, *pulusukāya*; in Tamil: *koššittamarattāi*, *pilimbi pulišsakāy*, *puḻimā*; in Malayalam: *bilimpi*, *karišsakka*, *vilumpi*; in Canarese: *bilimbi*, *bimbuli* (Lushington, *List*, 366; *cf.* also Yule-Burnell, s. v. *blimbee*. The note furnished by Yule and Burnell, s. v. *Carambola*, may be conveniently reproduced here; "Sir J. Hooker observes that the fact that there is an acid and a sweet-fruited variety (*blimbee*) of this plant indicates a very old cultivation.") But the evidence of Garcia de Orta, amongst others, shows clearly that for a competent connoisseur *karmaraṅga* and *bilimbi* are equivalent terms: "These carambolas are called in Canar and the Decan *camariz* and in Malaya *balimba*." (Yule-Burnell, s. v *Carambola*.) And Linschoten (*ibid*): "The fruit which the Malabaris and the Portuguese call Carambola is called *Camarix* in the Deccan, *Camarix* and *Carabeli* in Canara and *Bolumba* in Malay." Mevilimbaṅgam should, therefore, be analysed, in the inscription of Tanjore, like Mā-Damāliṅgam, Mā-Ṇakkavāram, as *Me-Vilimbaṅgam*; it is clear that *Vilimbaṅgam* is the Indian transcription of Malaya *belimbing* which is the equivalent of Karmaraṅga. The Indian name of the fruit derived from the name of the country, has become in its turn the indication of the country itself; Karmaraṅga has become the country of the carambol tree, and as can be seen in the list of the names borrowed from Lushington, the Malaya name of the fruit has made its way in all parts of South India along with the name given by Sanskrit. But then the identity of Kamalanka-Lĕṅkasuka is to be abandoned, because Lēnkasuka is clearly mentioned in the Inscription of Tanjore under its Tamilised form Ilangaśogam. The two countries are certainly very near each other, but they cannot be confounded and Māppapāḷam is probably to be located between them, as it is mentioned between the two names.

By the side of *Lang-kia (shu)* and symmetrical with *Ka(r)mal(r)aṅk(g)a* comes the name of *Tām(r)aliṅga,* with the alterance *k- t-* of which Kalinga-Tilinga, Kosala-Tosala have given us incontestable examples. Mr. Coedès has recognised the name in the inscription of Tanjore where it appears under the form *Mā-Damāḷiṅgam*; he has also discovered the same name, this time under the form of *Tāmbraliṅga,* in an inscription coming from Jaiya and now preserved in Bangkok. I have pointed out elsewhere that it is to be found in the Mahā-Niddesa under the form *Tambaliṅga* (*Ptolemée le Mahā-Niddesa et le Bṛhatkathā,* B. E. F. E. O., Jubilee collection). M. Coedès has also recognised the identity of this name with the country of *Tan-ma-ling* mentioned amongst the vassals of San-fo-t'si in the *Tchu fan tche* of Tchao. Ju kua (transl. Hirth and Rockhill, p. 62) and described in a special note (p. 67 ff.) immediately before *Ling-ya-sse* [*kia*], Laṅkasuka. Mr. Rockhill published later in (*T'oung Pao,* 1915, p. 123) another note on Tan-ma-ling taken from the *Tao yi tche liao*; Tan-ma-ling, according to this text, is adjacent to Sha-li Fu-lai-ngan; but the position of this last place is also uncertain (*cf.* Blagden, J. R. A. S., 1913, p. 166). M. Coedès, after considering all the previous opinions concludes with probability that the country of Tāmaliṅga certainly covered Jaiya and most probably Nagor Sri Dharmaraj. As regards the name Tāmbralinga written in the inscription of Jaiya, M. Coedès observes: "*Tāmbra* is a Prakritic form of *tāmra*, copper, still used in Singhalese. The meaning of the expression Tāmralinga is not very clear. Taking *liṅga* in the sense of mark or character, Tāmralinga could signify (the country) which has copper as its characteristic, but I do not believe that copper has ever been reported in the north of the Malaya peninsula. It can be supposed also that the country derived its name from a 'linga of copper' which had some celebrity." Probably copper has no more to do with this name than with most of the other place-names where Sanskrit has *tāmra*; we shall explain this later on in connection with the name of Tāmralipti.

The alternation of the preformatives *kam-tam*, which we believe to have recognised in the names of *Kam-ləng*= Kamalaṅka, Karmaraṅga, Kāmaraṅga, etc., and of *Tam-ləng*=Tāmraliṅga, etc., appears to be reproduced on the very soil of India, in the region where we have already noticed some ethnic couples differentiated only by the preformatives. *Kāmarūpa* and *Tāmralipti* seem to furnish a new example.

The word *kāmarūpa*, considered from the standpoint of Sanskrit, is a regular compound, in current use, of which the meaning is perfectly clear: *kāma*, desire+*rūpa* form. The association of the two words is not at all strange as the Buddhist cosmology distinguishes in the universe the world of *kāma*, *kāmadhātu* and the world of *rūpa*, *rūpadhātu*. The use of the term of *kāmarūpa* in literature constantly indicates the faculty of metamorphosing at will. As regards the country of Kāmarūpa, though it is not mentioned in the epics, which include it in Prāgjyotiṣa, Kālidāsa names it (*Raghuv.*, IV, 84); in the time of Harṣa Śīlāditya, it was a first class state in Indian politics, and had relation with China. Owing specially to Tantrikism Kāmarūpa has enjoyed a durable popularity; this is a *pīṭha*, a sacred place, where one of the relics of the Devī was adored. The Yoginītantra, paṭala XI (quoted in *Ep. Ind.*, XII, 68) traces the frontier of Kāmarūpa thus:

*Nepālasya Kāñcanādriṁ Brahmaputrasya saṁgamam*
*Karatoyaṃ samārabhya yāvad Dikaravāsinīm*
*uttarasyāṁ Kañjagiriḥ Karatoyā tu paścime*
*tīrthaśreṣṭhā Dikṣunadī pūrvasyāṁ Girikanyake*
*dakṣiṇe Brahmaputrasya Lākṣāyāḥ saṁgamāvadhi*
*Kāmarūpa iti khyātaḥ sarvaśāstreṣu niścitaḥ*

"From the mountain Kāñcana in Nepal up to the confluence of the Brahmaputra, from the Karatoyā to Dikkara-Vāsinī, the northern limit is the mount Kañja; in the west the Karatoyā, in the east the Dikṣu (Oh, daughter of the mountains), in the south the confluence of the Lākṣā with the Brahmaputra; this is the territory which all the treatises call by the name of Kāmarūpa."

The official nomenclature still continues to designate the western part of Assam by the name of Kamrup. But, in the religious sense, Kāmarūpa also includes Bhutan, Kuch Behar and Rangpur. The temple of Kāmākhyā, near Gauhati, is considered to be the mystical centre. It is a mountainous region where one finds all the dialects of India: of Aryan, Muṇḍā, Tibeto-Burman, and Mon-Khmêr families. At the time of Hiuan-tsang's visit

King Bhāskaravarman, was "a descendant of the God Nārāyaṇa"; he was "of the caste of the Brahmaṇas," and had the title of "Kumāra." "Since the possession of the kingdom by his family up to his time, the succession of princes covers a space of a thousand generations" (*Mém.* II, 77.) The evidence of his contemporary Bāṇa (*Harṣacarita*, chap. VII) confirms almost all these details. Finally we possess since a few years ago an inscription of King Bhāskaravarman (Nidhanpur plates, *Ep. Ind.*, XII, 65), which takes back the genealogy up to King Bhagadatta, the famous adversary of the Pāṇḍavas, by a long list of ancestors. However, when he had business with others than Indians, the same prince boasted of another origin altogether. When the envoy of the T'ang dynasty, Li Yi-piao, paid him a visit during the course of his mission (643-646) the king in a private conversation, told him: "the royal family has handed down its power for 4,000 years. The first was a holy spirit which came from China (*Han-ti*) flying through the air" (*She-kia fang tche*, ed. Tok. XXXV, 1, 94b, *col. ult.*). As though he would show sympathy for China, he asked the envoy to get him a portrait of Lao-tseu and a Sanskrit translation of the *Tao-tö-king*. The Emperor, on his part, wished to respond to this desire and promulgated an edict asking the master of the Law, Hiuan-tsang, to prepare the translation in collaboration with Taoist teachers (*cf.* on this episode the article of M. Pelliot: *Autour d'une traduction Sanscrite du Tao-tö king in T'oung-pao*, Vol. XIII, 1912, p. 351 ff.). After the dynasty of Bhāskaravarman, Kāmarūpa never ceased to be subject to barbarian races who have been gradually Hinduized. The best known period is that of the Ahoms, of the Tai or Shan race, which succeeded in creating a kind of original civilisation and in maintaining their power from the 13th to the 19th century.

The Brahmins have naturally invented a legend to explain the name of Kāmarūpa : it is there that *Kāma*, Love, sent by the gods to put an end to Śiva's mourning after the death of his wife, and to awaken in him again the tender passion, was burnt by an angry look of Śiva and then recovered his original form (*rūpa*). By the side of this childish explanation, it will suffice to state that the easternmost province of the kingdom of Assam, on the very confines of Burma, bore the name of Namrup ; Namrup was on the other side of the Dikhu, which marks the religious limit of Kāmarūpa on the East, midway between this river and the Upper Chindwin, in a hardly accessible region which has always served as a shelter for the vanquished. The climate there is deadly ; an Assamese proverb, quoted by Gait (*History of Assam*, p. 144) says that if a bird flies over the country, the bats get back their lives, and if steel enters into the soil, it will change into wax. A Brahman would not have felt any difficulty in interpreting the name Namrup as Nāmarūpa, a compound so natural and so familiar that it would seem to suggest itself spontaneously : *Nāma-rūpa*, name and form, are the essential categories into which existence is resolved. But the Philosophy of the Upaniṣads is out of place in this wild corner and the Metamorphoses still more so in Kāmarūpa. We have here "barbarous" names in which the same element noted as *rup* and Sanskritised as *rūpa*, is associated with pre-formatives *kam* and *nam*. It would not, therefore, appear strange if we discover the same element with the pre-formative *tam* formed with the prefix *ka* regularly increased by nasal. It is this combination which appears to me to be at the root of the name of Tāmralipti.

Tāmralipti was for centuries the greatest port of the Bay of Bengal. It is there that the missions exchanged between Aśoka and the King of Ceylon embarked and disembarked (*Mahāvaṁsa* XI, 38 ; XIX, 6). Fa-hien embarked there for Ceylon ; Yi-tsing disembarked there when coming from China and it is there also that he embarked for Śrīvijaya in Sumatra. The city, on account of its importance, is frequently mentioned in stories ; the Mahābhārata also mentions, very often, the city, the kingdom, and the king, *e.g.* I, 186, 6993 ; II, 29, 1098 ; 51, 1874 ; VI, 9, 364 ; VII, 70, 2436 ; 119, 4716...The Jaina Prajñāpanā calls the city the capital of Vaṅga in the list of the *āriyas* of the first order, the *khettariya* which we have already quoted many times : *Rāyagiha Magaha Campā Aṁga taha Tāmalitti Vaṁga ya* (*Ind. St.*, XVI, 397). The Daśakumāra (story of Mitragupta) makes it a city of Suhma. It commanded the entrance and the exit of the river Ganges. To-day, it is a market-town with some thousands of souls, called Tamluk, on the Rupnarayan, not far from its confluence with the Hughli. It is strange that the name of such a famous city has never taken a definite form. The dictionary of Hemcandra quotes (V. 979) four forms of the name : *Tāmaliptā, Dāmalipta, Tāmaliptī, Tamālinī*, and besides two surnames : *Stambapūr* and *Viṣṇugṛha* ; the Trikāṇḍaśeṣa (2, 1, 11) adds *Tāmālikā*. The Śabdakalpadruma adds even another *Tamoliptī*. To all these designations we must add another which is met with the most often, *Tāmralipta* (°*ā*, °*ī*). In almost all the passages, the manuscripts hesitate and the two forms *tāmra* and *tāma* are alternately given in the same text. The Chinese pilgrims transcribe *To-mo-li-ti* [1] (Fa-hien), or *Tan-mo-li-ti* [2] (Hiuan-tsang) and *Tan-mo-li-li* [3] (Yi-tsing). Ptolemy (VII, 1, 76) writes Tamalitēs. MacCrindle (*Ind. Ant.*, XIII, 364) has compared Tamalitēs with the name of *Taluctoe* mentioned by Pliny, VI, 18, on this side of India. The name of Tāmraliptī seems to have been transported to Cambaye in the course of the middle ages: the *Pañcadaṇḍachattraprabandha* (ed. Weber, § 3) begins one of its tales with: *Stambhatīrthe Tāmaliptyāṁ Jayakarṇabhūpagṛhe* "in Cambay, at Tāmraliptī, in the palace of the King Jayakarṇa;" and the Siṁhāsanadvātriṁśika (*Ind. Stud.*, XV, 252) begins with the history of a king Tāmraliptarṣi who lives in Gujrat, between the Sabarmati and the Mahi (*Gurjarimaṇḍale Sābhravatī-Mahilānadyor antare vanaṁ vidyate tatra rājā Tāmraliptarṣiḥ*). Weber says in his note on this passage (*Pañcad.*, p. 71) that Cambaye bears also the name of *Tāmravatī*, or *Trāmbavatī* from Guzerati *trambuṁ* = Sk. *tāmra* "copper" because according to the legend, the city had in ancient times a wall of copper. Weber does not give the reference; he probably got his information from Bühler, who is quoted in the notice on Cambaye. It is probable that the name of Stambapūr, given as synonym of Tāmralipti by Hemacandra, applied in reality to Cambaye, the Sanskrit name of which is *Stambha-tīrtha*—Prakrit *Khambha*. Fancy has been given a free play on these numerous variants. The *Imperial Gazetteer of India*,[1] *s. v.* Tamluk, writes

[1] 多摩梨帝 [2] 呾摩栗底

[3] 耽摩立底

"The very name of the city points to its ancient unorthodox character; but it has been so cleverly manipulated that it has at last become a title of honour. The Grammarians derive the word from *tamo* (*tamas*)-*lipta*, 'tainted by obscurity or sin.' But a legend relates that Viṣṇu, under the form of Kalki, having got heated in destroying the demons, let his sweat fall on the earth, and the place which was fortunate enough to receive this sacred perspiration derived its name from that and became a holy place" (*tāma* "fatigue" + *lipta*). All these pretended etymologies show once more the uncertainty and the embarrassment of the interpreters. Tamālinī, Tamālikā are hopeless efforts to find a meaning out of this mysterious groups of syllables; one has tried to discover there the name of the tree *tamāla*, *Xanthochymus pictorius* (Lushington, *List*, n. 178). The Jaina Bhagavatī in the second śataka tells the story of a Moriyàputta of Tāmalitti who called himself *Tāmali* and seems to have been the object of a local cult. Copper, *tāmra*, appears to have discouraged the exegetists, who, however, could have given to Tāmralipti also, as to Tāmravatī = Cambaye, the walls "coated with copper." One sees now how futile it would be to attempt a literal interpretation of so many geographical names of India with *tāmra*, as the first element. The list is infinite; the most famous case is the name of Ceylon, *Tāmraparṇī*, *Tāmbraparṇī* or *Taprobanē* of the Greeks. If copper has sometimes its *raison d'être* there, in most cases it only reveals an ancient prefix *tam* placed at the beginning of old denominations; such is the case with Tāmralinga, Tāmalinga, Təm(bə)ləng, which we have considered above.

If the first element of Tām(r)alipti can be thus explained, it may not be impossible that the second *lip*, corresponds to *rūp*, becoming in Sanskrit *rūpa*, from Kamrup =Kāmarūpa. The kingdom of Tāmralipti almost bordered on Kāmarūpa : To pass from one to the other Hiuan-tsang had only to traverse the small kingdom of Samataṭa. The river which waters Tamluk, the *Rūpa*-Nārāyaṇa seems to preserve in the first element of the compound the pre-Aryan word which appeared also in the name of the country. The correspondence *i*(*lip*)= *u*(*rup*) is possible ; the modern name Tamluk seems to have preserved the timbre of the real vowel, altered in the Sanskrit adaptation. (The final *k* of Tamluk, substituted for *p* of *rup*, is normal in the present domain of Tibeto-Burmans ; at the time of writing this, I receive the *Report of the Superintendent, Archaeological Survey, Burma*, 1923 ; on page 23, I find that the saint Upagupta of Sanskrit Buddhism is venerated in Burma under the name of Upagok). The name of Śrīvijaya, now put again in full light, shows constantly an identical alteration ; the Chinese transcriptions always render the Sanskrit syllable *vi* by the character which designates Buddha and of which the pronunciation *bud* is not doubtful. The timbre *u*(*o*) is still preserved in the Arabic transcription Sribuza, Serboza. On the opposite border of the vast domain of Indian civilisation, the name of *Kapiśa* (*Capisa quam diruit Cyrus* in Pliny, VI. 92), becomes in the Tibetan translation of the Mahā-Māyūrī : *ka. bu. śa.* The identity Kapiśa=Kabuśa leads to the question whether it can extend to Kamboja also. It is surprising, in fact, to observe that according to the Chinese documents, the rôle of Kapiśā seems to have been of the first importance for India in politics and religion, while its name, so to say, is hardly ever met with in Indian literature. The Mahā Bhārata which is so well acquainted with the North-West of the Indian world, does not mention Kapiśā even once, while the name of Kamboja appears there almost incessantly. Kamboja and Kapiśā seem to be two attempts to render the same foreign word in a language which did not lend itself to the purpose : $\frac{ka}{kam} = k\text{ə}m$ ; of $\frac{p}{b}$ $\frac{\acute{s}}{j}$ each has a labial followed by a palatal, unvoiced in the first case and sonant in the second ; the middle term seems to have been in the two cases a spirant : *f* and *z* both of which are wanting in Sanskrit. The spirant appears in Greek also, in the sibilant of the proper name Kambysēs = Ka(n)buǰiya, the son of Cyrus, of whom the name probably recalled one of the conquests of his father, the destructor of Kapiśā. In any case, the two spirants seem to be quite clear in the title of *Kadphizēs* claimed by the Kushans, when their power had spread from the district of *Kuei-shuang* to that of *Kao-fu* = *Kambu* in Chinese transcription. The title of Kadphizēs is symmetrical with the title of Taxilēs, under which the king of Taxila-Takṣaśilā whose personal name was Ambhi, is famous in the history of Alexander. Both are *tadrāja*, according to the terminology of Pāṇini, IV, I, 174 ; Kamboja has even the honour of a special sūtra, IV, 1, 175, *kambojāl luk* : there is no Vṛddhi for designating the king ; he is *Kāmboja* (and not *Kamboja*). It is an exception which *Kātyāyana* and *Patañjali* extends to a series of princes : Coḍa, Kaḍera, Kerala and which Candragomin, II, 4, 104, completes with Śaka, all "margraves," chiefs established on the borders of India. I do not want to push this complicated question further here. I propose to take it up again elsewhere in detail with a view to drawing certain conclusions that bear on the history of the Kushans in particular. I will quote here only one case which is very characteristic of the alternation Kapiśā-Kamboja. The Rāmāyaṇa, in the Kashmirian recension (Weber, *Ramayana*, p. 95 note), reads in the verse IV, 44, 23, *Āraṭṭaṁ Kapiśaṁ Bālhīṁ*. Kṣemendra, in his Mañjarī (iv. 252), writes *Āraṭṭa Bālhi Kāmboja°*. Between the *i* of Kapiśa and the *o* of Kamboja, the intermediary appears to be a soft *u*, analogous to the French *u*, which Sanskrit does not possess and which is supposed by the alternation of (*Śrī*) *vi* (*jaya*) and of (*She-li*)-*fo* (=*bu*[d]) (*she*) in the Indonesian domain. In precisely the same domain, we find a name analogous to but not identical with Kamboja; it is *Kam-vuja*, the present Cambodge, which the Singhalese and the Tibetans have equally made *Kamboja*, but which never appears with an *o* in the epigraphic texts written on the spot. *Kam-vuja* seems to make a counterpart of Śrī-vija(ya), and specially of the form transcribed by *San-fo-ts'i* (=*Sam-bu*[d]-*jay*) in Chinese and noted as *semboja* in Javanese (for different forms of this name *cf.* Ferrand, J. A., 1919, II, 158). Schlegel (*T'oung-pao*, II, 176) had already supposed the relation between *Kemboja* and *Semboja*, in which he found the Malay name of the *Plumeria acutifolia*; but it is a plant of recent importation, a native of central America and now spread over India and Indonesia (Lushington, *List*, 1825; Pagoda tree: Jasmine spurge; Spanish American Jasmine); the names which it has received in Uriya (*gōsampige*), and in Tulu (*gosampige*; *sampāi*) are manifestly related with the Malay name. If the relation between Kamboja and Sambojā be exact, it will be necessary to go back still further to explain it. It may be then questioned whether the name at the bottom is not that of the *Bhoja*, which it is true, has an aspirate initial; but the analogy of the words *bhojana*, *bhoga* and others derived from the root *bhuj* in Sanskrit was strong enough to introduce this alteration. The Bhojas have been admitted to an elevated rank in Brahmanical society, on account of their alliance with Kṛṣṇa; the Mahā Bhārata in which they often appear generally associates them with the Vṛṣṇi and the Andhaka, the two principal clans of the party of Kṛṣṇa. But Aśoka classes them still amongst the frontier countries (Edict, XIII) on the same footing with the Yavana and the Kamboja. The geography of the Purāṇas (*Mārk.*, 57, 53; *Vāyu*, 45, 132; *Matsya*; 113, 52) classes them amongst the populations of the Vindhyas where they are found with the Kosala, Tosala, Utkala, etc.[1] In modern times the name Bhoja became more familiar than that of Kamboja and reacted on the

[1] By a singular chance, the name of Kamboja and that of Cambodge present, independently and at a very long interval, the same alteration of the initial. Ptolemy, VI, 11, 6 when describing Bactriane, places to the south of the Oxus the *Tambyzoi* by the side of the *Tokharoi*; it is not at all doubtful that *Tambyzoi* is here the equivalent of *Kamboja* as *Tokharoi* of *Tukhāra*.

On the other hand the name of Cambodge has undergone in China a final transformation or rather deformation at the beginning of the 17th century; the name (of *Kan-po-tche*) becomes there *Tong-pu-tch'ai* (Pelliot, *B.E.F.E.O.*, II, 126). Prof. Pelliot proposes to consider the character which is read as *tong* as faulty and to substitute for the character 柬 whichi as *kien*. It is not perhaps a mere chance; the initial *k*, becoming palatalised has in both the cases changed into a dental.

To note further that one of the mouths of the Ganges, the westernmost, bears in Ptolemy, VII, 1. 18 & 30 the name of *Kambuson*.

latter. The last dynasty of Vijaynagar, in the 16th century, regularly couples the two names : its princes pride themselves of being honoured by *Kāṁbhoja-Bhoja-Kaliṅga*, etc. See for example *Ep. Ind.* XI, 334 ; XII, 343 ; XIII, 229, XVI, 313. The name of Kamboja is always written there as *Kāṁbhoja* in imitation of *Bhoja*. The pandits of Vijayanagar could have produced in support of their spelling an almost sacred authority ; the grammarian Yāska, the predecessor of Pāṇini, in the famous passage of the Nirukta, II, 1, 4, where he mentions the use of the verb *śav* in the sense of "going" amongst the Kamboja adds a curions interpretation of the name : *śavatir gatikarmā Kambojeṣv eva bhāṣyate Kambojāḥ Kambalabhojāḥ kamanīya-bhojā vā kambalah kamanīyo bhavati*... "The Kamboja, these are "Bhojas with the mantle of wool (*kambala*)," or "the Kamboja as *kamanīya* (desirable)" ; the desirable (for them), is a mantle of wool (on account of the cold, adds a gloss)." Yāska gives this etymology in order to show clearly the position of the Kambojas in relation to the Āryas, whose linguistic usage he opposes to that of the Kambojas in the following sentence ; the Kamt-boja, as they are a branch of the Bhoja, do not form a part of the Ārya. Thus, at an ancient epoch close to what is called the Vedic period, an erudite and sagacious grammarian analyses the name of the Kambojas, as we propose to do, into *kam + bhoja* and he frankly admits his difficulty in explaining by Sanskrit the element *Kam* placed at the head of the name.

After this long digression, my attempt to discover in Tāmalipti a correspondance with the name Kāmarūpa may perhaps not seem so daring. Besides, I do not pretend to put forward anything except a hypothesis for discussion. Whatever may be the final issue, it would not affect the conclusions of our work. These pairs of ethnics, identical in form, differentiated only by their initial, apply to regions placed by couples in close juxtaposition. The process of differentiation by an initial preformative is foreign to the two groups of languages, Aryan and Dravidian, which have created the civilisation of historic India. It is characteristic of a family of languages, which is even to-day spread over a vast domain, from the Himalayas to the Island of Palks, and which still maintain themselves in the hills in the interior of India. The later representatives of this ancient race are the unconscious inheritors of a civilisation which had its greatness. It had created in India veritable political units of a considerable extent, so strongly linked with the real life of the country that they have continued to exist across the millenniums up to our days. The parallel existence of these twin ethnics, as it were, sometimes they are triplets, throws a curious light on the political and social constitution of this civilisation. Mr. James Hornell, in a brilliant essay on the origin and the ethnological signification of the Indian boats (*Memoirs of the Asiatic Society of Bengal*, Vol. VII, n° 3, 1920) has been led by his researches of a technical character to conclusions which he had to accept he says, though he was not prepared for them, and these conclusions are not without analogy with ours. He admits a strong Polynesian influence on the Pre-Dravidian population of the Southern coast of India: a wave of Malayan immigration must have arrived later, after the entrance of the Dravidians on the scene, and it was they who brought from the Malaya Archipelago the cultivation of the cocoa-tree. I still recall, as a sort of excuse for my boldness, that the erudite and inventive A. Weber was not afraid to point out the possible relation between an unexplained word, which remains still inexplicable, *tābuvam*, which he had met with in the Veda of Magic (Atharvav.; V, 13) in a formula against the poison of serpents and the Australo-Polynesian word *tabou* (*Sitzb. Ak. Wiss. Berlin*, 1876, XXXI, p. 684); he thought of a late borrowing, coming from India by way of the Indian colonies of Indonesia. Barth, when criticising this Memoir in the *Bulletin des Religions de l'Inde* (*Œuvres*, II, p. 254), reasonably observed: "It attaches a very great fortune to three obscure syllables lost in a corner of the Atharvaveda"; he added nevertheless: "If there be a relation between the two words, it would be rather, as it seems to me, in the inverse sense." There is occasion now to take the question up again and to pursue a methodical research to disclose the influences which this past had exercised on the development of Indian civilisation. Prof. Przyluski has already boldly opened the way for the vocabulary (*Mém. Soc. Ling.*, XXII, 205, *Bull. Soc. Ling.*, XXIV, 118 ff.). We must know whether the legends, the religion and the philosophical thought of India do not owe anything to this past. India has been too exclusively examined from the Indo-European standpoint. It ought to be remembered that India is a great maritime country, open to a vast sea forming so exactly its Mediterranean, a Mediterranean of proportionate dimensions—which for a long time was believed to be closed in the south. The movement which carried the Indian colonisation towards the Far East, probably about the beginning of the Christian Era, was far from inaugurating a new route, as Columbus did in navigating towards the West. Adventurers, traffickers and missionaries, profited by the technical progress of navigation and followed, under the best conditions of comfort and efficiency, the way traced from time immemorial, by the mariners of another race, whom the Aryan or Aryanised India despised as savages. The daring and skill of these men she was unable to appreciate before and she continued to ignore all that she owed to them.

# APPENDIX

TO

PART I.

## FURTHER NOTES ON NON-ARYAN LOANS IN INDO-ARYAN

BY

JEAN PRZYLUSKI.

# I

# Non-Aryan Loans in Indo-Aryan

## SANSKRIT *Mātaṅga* [1]

The elephant is capable of taking objects by its trunk. This is why in some languages its name is derived from the word signifying "hand." In Sanskrit *hastin*, *karin*, "elephant" means an animal which has a hand (*hasta-*, *kara-*). In a part of the Indonesian group, *liman* is a name of elephant derived from *lima* "hand."

In the Austro-Asiatic languages the words which mean 'hand' fall under two principal types: with or without the final consonant.

(*a*) With the final consonant; dialects of the Malay peninsula: *tong*, *tung*, *tāk* (*cf.* Khmer *dang* [*ṭang*]; Stieng *tōng* "the wrist, handle").

(*b*) Without the final consonant: Mon *toa* [*tai*]; Khmer *day* [*ṭai*]; Annamite *tay*; Palaung *tai*; Santali *ti*, etc.

It is probable that all these forms originated from an ancient *taṅ* (Skeat and Blagden had already proposed *tañ* with reservation) as in the Austro-Asiatic languages a final consonant often disappears and yields place to a vocalic element *i* and *y*. It is thus that one

[1] Jean Przyluski, *Bulletin de la Société de Linguistique*, 1925 (79), pp. 98-103.

may explain the forms like Malay and Batak *taṅan* ; Malagashy *tåṅan* ; Čam *taṅin* ; Jarai *töṅan*, all of which mean "hand."

Some of the dialects of the Malay peninsula for designating 'elephant' has a word with the element *taṅ*, *toṅ* : *tangäl*, *maiṇtong*.

If some of the details of these modern forms are very obscure, the case is different with Indo-Aryan *mātaṅga* "elephant." One can discover there, at the first sight, the element *taṅ* preceded by the prefix *ma*. *Mātaṅga-*, which is thus the name of an animal, is also used sometimes to mean an aboriginal tribe of India, as it very often happens (*cf.* Oldenberg, *La religion du Véda*, trans. Henry, p. 71, 72).

The existence of a prefix *ma-* in the Austro-Asiatic languages is proved specially by the following example : it is found in Santali *maraṅ* which A. Campbell translates as "great, large, big, huge, to become or cause to become great, large, big, huge ; first-born, principal, head, chief" ; *maraṅ* is derived from a root *raṅ*, *laṅ* and a prefix *ma-* as is indicated by the words which mean "great" in languages of the same family : Čam, *prauṅ*, Jaraï *proṅ*, *gloṅ*. In modern Annamite *lớn* "great" has only preserved the root. But the middle Annamite *mlớn* still preserved, in the 17th century, the trace of the element *ma*.

In Khasi a particle of emphasis *ma-* is placed before the pronouns. "*Ma-* prefixed emphasises the pronoun ; *ngā la ong*, *ma - ngā*=I said, even I" (*Linguistic Survey of India,* II, p. 9). It even seems that this particle of emphasis used in polite forms before the pronoun of the second person exists in a contracted form along with it.

In face of Bahnar *ē*, *īḥ*, Kaseng and Halang *ai* "you, thou," there is in Kon-tu and Sué *mai*, and in Annamite *mày* or *mäy* which have the same meaning, In Stieng two different forms either with or without *m*, exist side by side for specific use; *éi* is used when speaking to a woman and *mĕi* when addressing a man.

SANSKRIT *mayūra-*, *mayūka-*, *marŭka-*.

A name of peacock *mayūra-* already appears in the Ṛgveda. Prof. Jules Bloch has recently compared it with Dravidian, Munda and Indo-Chinese forms (B S.L. XXV, p. 16). The principal Austro-Asiatic forms are the following:

| | |
|---|---|
| Santali | *marak'* |
| Savara | *mara* |
| Čam | *amrak* |
| Malay | *mera* |
| Črau | *brak* |
| Stieng | *brăk* |
| Mon | *mrā* |

Most of these words present a final guttural and the ancient form seems to have been *marak* preserved almost intact in Santali where *k'* is the notation of implosive. In *marak* the prefix *ma* can be isolated from the root *rak* which imitates the cry of this bird. In fact in the Santali dictionary of A. Campbell the following word is found.

*rak'* "to weep, to beseech, the call, cry or note of a beast, bird or insect."

Amongst the examples given under this word we have: *marak' rak'* "peacock-crow which is earlier than cock-crow."

The same syllable *rak* explains Malay *sorak*, Khmer *srek* and Jarai *kraih*, all of which mean "to cry." The peacock, of which the shrill cry is heard before that of the cock is the bird that cries *rak*. In Sanskrit a name of peacock is *marŭka* which is formed after the Austro-Asiatic word, if one accepts the equivalence *a*=*u* of which I have already given examples in a previous article (B. S. L. XXIV, p. 120).

Besides *marŭka-* another name of peacock in Sanskrit is *mayūka* mentioned in the supplement of the dictionary of Hemacandra. The change of the first into the second of these forms can be easily explained in the Austro-Asiatic languages. It is thus that we have in Malay *merah*, Čam *möriah*, and Jarai *miyăḥ* for the adjective "red."

*Mayūka* and *mayūra*, which have the same meaning are so much similar to each other that nobody is justified in separating them. Moreover, one feels tempted to think of their relationship because *-ka* and *-ra* are regular suffixes in Indo-Aryan. But how has one passed from the one form to the other? The Vedic language, learned and aristocratic, has transposed the popular word, and images to a higher plane; it is just the cause of its obscurity and prestige. *Mayūka-* borrowed from the aboriginal tribes was of too humble an origin to be used in the Vedic hymns for the most noble bird. Was it possible to change the termination? *Mayūka-* had the appearance of being formed from *mayū*+*ka-*.[1] In substituting *-ka* by *-ra* an unexpected and consequently less popular aspect was

[1] The Indo-Aryans were accustomed to this kind of arbitrary analysis. The word *sura*—'god,' for instance, has been created in an unjustified manner by isolating the initial *a* from *asura*.

given to the word. Perhaps the suffix *-ra* was also more respectable than *-ka* as it opposed its popular equivalent *-la.*

*Mayūra-*, once admitted into the religious literature, had evolved like other Indo-Aryan words. The existence of a Prakrit form *mora* explains the name of the *Maurya* dynasty. This word which the Chinese translators render by "the family of the Peacock" is to be classed with *Mātaṅga* amongst the names of tribes and royal clans related to animal or vegetable of which the list will grow with the progress in our research.

Thus the prefix *ma-*, which we have discovered in Santali *maraṅ* and in several Austro-Asiatic pronouns is found again at the beginning of the names of "elephant" and "peacock." The elephant, the lord of the forest, and the peacock, the king of birds, occupy a high place in the order of beings; *maraṅ* qualifies that which is either physically or morally great; in Khasi the particle *mā-* is emphatic. To what extent is the element *ma* a real prefix? Is it not rather an element of vocabulary, a word having an augmentative value? In a large number of Indo-Chinese and Indonesian languages *mas* or *mah* is a name of gold, the precious metal *par excellence*. In Javanese the same word *mas* which means 'gold' is also a title of noblese. In Stieng *mah* means 'great' and in Bahnar there is *mah* "gold" and *mā* "straight, the right side."

The problem only can be indicated here as it presents itself almost in the same manner as other prefixes. Thus the prefix *tam* which we have found out in Indo-Aryan *tāmbūlam* "betel" (B. S. L. XXIV, p. 256), normally precedes the names of trees in Stieng and Bahnar, is used in the languages of the same family to form the name of 'tree': *tam-loṅ, töm-loṅ, tom-chǐ* etc......and is in Khmer and in Stieng, under the forms *döm* [*ṭöm*], *töm*, a real name which means "trunk of a tree, principle, origin."

### SANSKRIT *makuṭa-*, *mukuṭa*.

As soon as we admit that in certain words the existence of prefix *ma-* had probably the augmentative value and was susceptible to take the form *mu-* we can try to analyse in the same way other Indo-Aryan words suspected to have been borrowed from the Austro-Asiatic languages. It will be seen later on that *makuṭa-*, *mukuṭa-* "diadem" contain the same prefix *ma-*, *mu-*. *Murala*, the name of a fish is also the name of a people (*Kathāsaritsāgara*, 19, 96), which has been assimilated to Kerala (Dict. of Saint-Petersburg under *murala*); besides *Murala* or *Murandalā* is the name of a river in the country of Kerala. We have here a play of suffixes and infixes which denotes an Austro-Asiatic origin. From *kerala-* one passes to *murala* by a substitution of the prefix *mu-* for *ke-* and *murandalā* is derived from *muralā* by the infixation of *nd*, a double infix frequent in the Austro-Asiatic languages. In supposing that *ma-*, *mu-* has here too the augmentative value it can be understood why this prefix has been used for designating a river, a people or an important tribe and the fish eponymous with this tribe. One may be even tempted to explain in the same way Vedic *marut*, name of wind, of the wind-gods and of the tempest, of which no satisfactory explanation has as yet been given. If the peacock **maruk*(*a*) is "the bird that cries," could not the wind and the Maruts be called "those who cry" or the "roarers"? In one of the Sakai dialects (Malay peninsula) *parug* is the word for wind with which one may compare, in the same region, *rū* "roar" (like a tiger) and Môn *pŭru* "roaring, sound." It is true that we have in Sanskrit *marut* and not **maruk*, but there is in Indo-Aryan a root *rud* meaning precisely "to cry, to lament, to roar" and the nouns like *rutam* "cry" and Rudra "the roarer," name of the great god, the chief of the Maruts. It might be conceived that by analogy with *rud*, *rutam*, the name of wind became *marut*. But here is merely a conjecture. The study of the proper names in Indo-Aryan cannot yield in many cases definite results so long as we ignore the importance of Austro-Asiatic contributions to the religion and civilisation of ancient India.[1]

---

[1] Before publishing such a comprehensive study I have begun to show in two monographs the influence of the Austro-Asiatic civilisation on the religious and social institutions of ancient India: *Études Asiatiques*, *La princesse à l'odeur de poisson et la nâgī dans les traditions de l'Asie orientale* and *Journal Asiatique*, 1924, II, p. 101 ff. *Le prologue-cadre des Mille et une nuits et le theme du Svayaṁvara*.

# II

# Names of Indian Towns in the Geography of Ptolemy[1]

*Pura* is one of the words which mean "town" in Sanskrit and names of towns ending in *pura* were numerous in ancient India. It is, therefore, quite strange that we meet only two such names in the Tables of Ptolemy: Sêlampoura and Mapoura.[2] We find besides a town which is called in different manuscripts either Pentapolis or Mentapolis and this word may be a hellenised form of an Indian name ending in *pura*. The prologue of the *Śuka-saptati* mentions a town called Pañcapura and places there a family of Brâhmaṇas.[3] Pentapolis represents exactly Pañcapura. Pentapolis therefore is comparable to Pentagramma (Ptol. I, 57), which seems to stand exactly for Pañcagrāma. The federation of five villages (*pañcagrāmī*) are known to the law texts (Yājñavalkya, 2, 272). In Pentagramma only the first part of the name is Greek, but in Pentapolis the whole name is such. The hellenisation of some toponomies should not astonish us in a book which enumerates countries like Argyrâ

[1] Jean Przyluski, *Bulletin de la Société de Linguistique*, 1926 (83), pp. 218-229.

[2] I refer once for all to the edition and index of Mr. Renou, *La géographie de Ptolémée, L'Inde* (*VII*, 1.4), Paris, Champion, 1925.

[3] The same town is also mentioned in the 40th section of the work.

and Khrysê and islands like Heptanêsia and Trinêsia. We know on the oth er hand that some Indian towns were formed by agglomerations [1] and this fact justifies names like Pañcapura, Pañcagrâma.

By the side of names in *-pura* we find names of towns of the type Hippokoura, Barakoura. Koura was no doubt an Indian word meaning "town." The Mahābhārata mentions on several occasions the town of Dantakura and associates it with the name of the Kaliṅga people. It does not seem to be doubtful at all that Dantakura was "a geographical name either analogous to or identical with Dantapura," the town of the Kaliṅgas (S. Lévi: *Notes Indiennes* in *Journ. As.*, 1925, I, 48-55, *infra*, App. to Part III). Dantapura may mean "the city of elephant's tusks." The country of Kaliṅga was famous for its elephants (*Le Parinirvāṇa et les Funérailles du Buddha*, pp. 117-8). Dantakura being a designation analogous to Dantapura, it is tempting to suggest the equivalence: *pura* = *kūra* = town. It will be seen just now that this hypothesis explains a certain number of facts.

In names like Hippokoura, Barakoura, the intervocalic occlusive *k* can easily change into a sonant *g*. This is why we find in the Tables of Ptolemy another type in *-goura* by the side of that in *-koura*; Nagagoura, Souannagoura, Astagoura. Naga no doubt stands for *nāga* "dragon"; Souanna for *suvarṇa* (*cf.* Pali *suvaṇṇa*) "gold"; asta for *aṣṭa* "eight." Nagagoura was probably the city of *nāga* (*cf.* modern Nagpur); Sounnagoura, "the city of gold" and Astagoura a name with a numerical element at the beginning comparable to

[1] On the different agglomerations comprised under the sole name of Vaisāli, *cf. Uvāsagadasāo*, edit. R. Hoernle, fols. 1, n. 8.

Pentapolis, Pentagramma.[1] The manuscripts of Ptolemy mentions still another town called Gammogoura or Brammokoura. The last reading conveys an acceptable meaning. Brammokoura was doubtless the city of Brahma (*cf.* in Ptolemy the towns Brammê and Bramma and in Burma the famous Prome). The hypothesis *pura* = *kūra* thus becomes more probable.

I have shown elsewhere (*Journ. As.*, 1926, pp. 25-9) that in some Indian names the initial frequently disappears. This phenomenon explains the passage of *pura* or *kūra* to *ūra*. In fact the names of towns ending in -oura are numerous in Ptolemy: Poloperoura, Koreoura, Karoura, etc. Numerous are also the names with the termination -our. These names stand in the same relation to those in -oura as the modern names in *pur* to those in *pura*. Nagour for example is comparable to Nagpur and Nagaoura.

Besides the names in the Tables of Ptolemy ending in *-oura* and *-our* are not without equivalents in modern onomasticon. Cannanore or *Kaṇṇanūr* or *Kaṇṇūr*, for example, is the city (*ūr*) of Kṛṣṇa (*cf. Hobson-Jobson*, s.v.); and to this Dravidian word *ūr* "city" or "village" corresponds in Canarese *ūru* and in Tamil *ūra* (*Ling. Surv. Ind.* IV, pp. 325 & 679). It is also *à priori* possible that the names of cities in *-oura* and *-our* are derived from *pura* as well as *kūra*. The quantity of *ū* in the Dravidian word *ūra, uru, ur* makes us more inclined to admit the second alternative.[2]

To sum up, besides the Indo-Aryan words like *pura*, *grāma*, etc., the names of towns in the Tables of Ptolemy

[1] For the name of towns with "eight" as its first element, *cf.* *Aṭṭhakanagara* at Sanchi Inscr., No. 204, and in *Aṅguttara*, V. 342.

[2] We have *pūr* in Vedic but *pura* has always *u*.

have for their second element, a series of forms · *koura*, *goura*, *oura*, *our* which are interconnected with each other and can all be explained by the single word *kūra* meaning "city."

As it often happens, the results which we have just arrived at. raise new problems. If *pura* is Indo-Aryan, to which languages do *kūra* and other words of the series properly belong ? What is the origin of the word *kūra* ?

We have just seen that the word *Dantakūra* seems to be modelled after *Dantapura*. There are still two other forms. *Dandagula* in Pliny VI, 73, corresponds to *Dantakūra* and Professor Sylvain Lévi has precisely shown that *Paloura* is another term for *Dandagula* (*Notes Indiennes*, p. 53). We have thus four forms corresponding with each other: *Dantapura*, *Dantakūra*, *Dandagula*, *Paloura*. If we suggest the equivalence : *pura*=*kūra*=*gula*=oura=city—then it necessarily follows that :

*danta*=*danda*=*pal*=tusk of elephant.

Now it remains to be answered in which languages *pal* can mean "elephant's tusk." We have in the Austro-Asiatic family :

| | | | |
|---|---|---|---|
| Malay Peninsula | *bālā'*, | *bālā*, | *bal'* |
| Khmer | *phluk* | | |
| Stieng | *bluk* | | |
| Kaseng | *blok* | | |
| Sue | *bölö* | | |
| Halang | *milà* | | |
| Sedang | *bölà* | | |
| Jarai, Bahnar | *böla* | | |
| Cam | *bala* | | |
| Kon-tu | *palò* | | |

All these words mean "elephant's tusk" and are connected with a root *bal* which signifies "horn" in the Austro-Asiatic languages and hence, means of defence for the elephant. The example of Khmer: *phlŭk*<*bhlŭk* and Kon-tu: *palò* shows that the initial sonant *b* can be softened into a sound *p*, a fact which explains the form *pal* which has been taken out from Paloura.

It is true that the equivalence *pal* = "elephant's tusk" rests solely on the fact that *pal* represents Sanskrit *danta*. But *danta* signifies as well: tooth, tooth of elephant and ivory. The Dravidian languages have the following words for tooth (*Ling. Surv. Ind.*, IV, 650):—

| | |
|---|---|
| Telugu, Malayālam, Tamil | *pallu* |
| Kaikāḍi | *pella* |
| Korvī | *pell* |
| Canarese | *hallu* |
| Kurukh | *pall* |
| Goṇḍi | *pal* |

In Paloura the element *pal* can therefore be either a Dravidian word meaning tooth or an Austro-Asiatic word meaning "elephant's tusk."[1] If we consider only the first syllable of the word, nothing permits us to decide if Paloura is Dravidian or Austro-Asiatic

Whatever it may be, *Dantapura*, *Dantakūra*, *Dandagula* and *Paloura* are intimately related to each other. It seems probable that these four names were equivalent

[1] It may be interesting to compare with these words the name of elephant in the Semitic languages: Assyrian: *pilu*, Aramean: *pīl*, Arab: *fīl*. We know that there is frequent confusion between the words for elephant and "ivory." In Greek, for example, ἐλέφας, first meant "ivory." It is probable that Assyrian *pilu*, Aramean *pīl*, etc., are borrowed from the languages of India.

to each other and used in different dialects. These names reveal, along with the diversity of local speeches, a strange case of linguistic syncretism, because, if Dantapura is clearly Aryan, the other forms are at least partially non-Aryan ; *kūra* is not known to be an Aryan name, and we find it associated with Sanskrit *danta*. We have here the proof of intimate penetration between Aryan and non-Aryan vocabularies and also the indication of ethnical and cultural mixture.

It is moreover possible to go still deeper into the hierarchy of forms. When enumerating the towns between the Pseudostomos and the Baris, Ptolemy (VII, 1, 86) mentions, after different localities, Karoura, the royal city, and then other towns which do not merit this epithet, and amongst them, Arembour, Koureour, Dêlour, etc. After the interior cities of Pandiones, such as Tainour, Korindour, we find Modoura, the royal city of the Pandiôn, then other towns such as Akour, Kaliour, Eikour, and then Orthoura, a royal city and other cities like Abour, Nagour, etc. It appears that in a vast territory, Karoura, Modoura, Orthoura were the royal cities while the names in -our designate the ordinary agglomerations. This distinction does not certainly hold good for other regions of India. It ceases to be true for the Arouarnoi of whom Skopeloura, the only town in -oura is not at all a royal city but further on amongst the Maisôloi, the only city in -oura : Pitoura is precisely called a metropolis. It seems that in the largest part of the Dekhan, the cities in -oura had a special dignity superior to that of the towns in -our. These differences in the onomasticon should correspond to two cultural levels. The names in -oura were perhaps in use in the official language while the names in -our belonged to country speeches.

Though it seems probable that *pura, kūra, *gūra, ūra, ūr*, correspond to some distinct social levels it is not easy to define to which families of languages do these forms belong. Professor Sylvain Lévi has thus written about koura : "One is inclined to connect the final °*koura* in Hippokoura with °*kourai*, which seems to be a plural form, in the name Sōsikourai (VII, 1, 10), which certainly corresponds to Tuticorin ; here *kourai* is without any doubt the equivalent of the Tamil word *kuḍi*—place of habitation, town—(*cf*. the texts ; s.v. *Tuticorin* in *Hobson-Jobson* of Yule and Burnell). But the identity kūra= kourai is very doubtful." (*Notes Indienness*, p. 57.)

Let us observe that the final —*ai* is not certain. Some MSS. give °*oureri*, °*ouri*, °*ouroi*, etc., and M. Renou, who for the first part of the word has too hastily accepted the reading *Mosi*°, might have had even good reason to adopt the reading °*kouri* for the second part of the word—a form very near to Tamil *koḍi* "town." Besides Ptolemy mentions a town Prokouri and a market place Tarakori (VII, 4, 6 and 7) in Taprobane. I presume that names of this type should also be connected with Tamil *kuḍi* and modern Tuticorin. The existence of forms like *kuḍi, ūru, ūra, ūr* in Dravidian can explain modern names like Tuticorin, Travancore, Cannanore, etc. ; but there is nothing to prove that these forms are properly Dravidian. The words which mean "town" being essentially words pertaining to a civilisation are always suspected to have been borrowed by the less advanced people from their neighbours. It is therefore necessary to examine if other non-Aryan languages of India contain anything of that kind.

In the Munda languages we have the following words for village (*cf. Ling. Surv. Ind.*, IV, pp. 272-5) :

| | | | |
|---|---|---|---|
| Santali | *atō* | | |
| Mahle | *ātō* | Kurku | *āhu* |
| Mundari | *hā·ū* | | |
| Birhar | *hātō* | Savara | *gorjañ* |
| Dhangar | *hūtō* | | |

In this group of languages ancient **k* may become a sonant, soften itself to *h* and can even disappear completely. The above forms therefore authorise us to suggest an ancient **kātŭ* for "village."

In Indonesia, on the other hand the names of towns or villages ending in *kuta* are numerous. With reference to the circumstances, the meaning we should attribute to this word is that of "capital," "fortress," "town" or "village." In Java, *kuta* means "the court," "the royal habitation." To Malay and Achin *kuta* correspond Minangkabao *kŏtŏ* and Batak *huta* (*Encyclopædie Van Nederlandsch-Indië*, 2nd ed. s.v. *kota*) [1]

Thus the Munda terms seem to be derived from an ancient **kātŭ* and the Indonesian forms can be traced back to *kuta*. These two Austro-Asiatic types appear to be related to the verbs meaning: to close, to enclose, etc., all agglomerations, great or small being in ancient times protected by a hedge or a wall against pillage and enemy.

| | | |
|---|---|---|
| Čam | *karo'k* | "close, shut, enclose, cover" |
| | *karo'ḥ* | "closing, shutting" |
| Bahnar | *krŏn* | "closing, shutting" |

[1] It is naturally admitted that all these words are loans from Sanskrit (*kuṭa* "fortress"). So, many villages without any importance would be, consequently, ancient fortresses and would have partly an Indian name. But it will be just now seen that the problem is not so simple.

| | | |
|---|---|---|
| Jarai | *krö, kri* | —— |
| Stieng | *kötah* | "cover" |
| Annamite | *kh'it* | "close, envelope" |
| Old Javan. Mak. Sund. Malay | *kuruṅ* | "enclosed, shut, enchained, to be shut" |
| Tagal | *koloṅ* | " |
| Dayak | *kuroṅ* [1] | " |

The same vowel and consonant changes which we find in the form of these verbs are also observed in the nouns meaning "skin, bark, shell" in the same domain. We have on one hand, in common Indonesian *kulit* "skin, bark" [2] and on the other in the languages of the continent :

| | | | | |
|---|---|---|---|---|
| Čam | *kulit* | "skin" | *kaḍuḥ* | "bark" |
| Bahnar | *akar* | " | *ködah* | " |
| Sue | *sönkal* | | | |
| Tareng, Kaseng | *aṅkàr* | " | | |
| Kon-tu | | | | |
| Malay Peninsula | *kĕtŏk* | " | *kĕtong* | "scales (of fish)" |
| | *keto'* | " | *kĕtong* | "shell (of tortoise)" |
| | *geto* | " | *kĕto'* | "egg-shell" |

[1] We should still add to this series the verbs meaning "surround by a link":

| | | | |
|---|---|---|---|
| Bahnar | *kŏt,* | Malay | *ikat* |
| Stieng | *kot* | Malay Pen. | *jekŏd* |
| Sedang | *kŏt* | | *ĕ ĕkat* |
| Mon | *dŏkat* | | |

[2] *Cf.* Brandstetter; trans. Blagden, *Indonesian Linguistics*, p. 34.

The analogy between the verbs of the series "to enclose" and the substantives of the series "skin, bark" is manifest. There is nothing to be surprised. Whether we mean the skin of an animal, the bark of a tree, the shell of a tortoise or the scale of a fish we always think of a "cover" and this notion can naturally be explained by "enclosure." The same root can well serve to designate all enclosed agglomerations : cities, fortresses protected by ramparts or simple villages protected by a thick enclosure as can be still seen in the Far East. And thus can be explained Indonesian words like *kuta* "town, village," and no doubt, the Sanskrit words such as *kuḍya* "wall" and *kuṭa* "fortress." These last two words can be added to the already long list of Indo-Aryan words borrowed from the non-Aryan languages.

Thus if we were to sum up, from an ancient Austro-Asiatic root *kar, kur, kut* meaning "to enclose, to cover" were derived :

(*a*) in the tables of Ptolemy the series : *-koura, -goura, -oura, -our,*

(*b*) in Sanskrit *kūḍya* "wall," *kuṭa* "fortress,"

(*c*) numerous words meaning "town" or "village" in the Munda, Indonesian and Dravidian languages. [1]

Should we then locate that cultural and linguistic horizon, from which these words so important for the history of institutions are derived, in the trans-Gangetic India ? There are facts to show that it will be a mistake not to look at all towards the west.

Amongst the ancient peoples of the North-West of India are found the Bhadras of whom the capital Śākala

[1] It can be even asked if some Indo-Aryan and non-Aryan words meaning "house" do not belong to the same family. This question merits a separate discussion.

was also called Bhadraṁkara. I have shown elsewhere that the Bhadras were also called Bhadrakāra, as such was the name of their city.[1] If Bhadra be an ethnic name then Bhadraṁkara, name of the capital, can signify "the city of the Bhadras." We can thus separate, the element °*kāra* from the name of a city of which the other name Śākala suggests that it might have been founded by a population coming from the west.

In the same way as °*koura* often becomes °*goura* in the tables of Ptolemy °*kara* also can be represented by numerous words ending in °*gara* : Mandagara, Armagara, Bramagara, Margara, Kamigara, Kattigara, etc.[2]

This new type largely surpasses the frontier of India. Mr. Autran points out to me the ancient names of cities in **kara* and **gara* in the west of India. Sumerian precisely contains a root which can explain these names.[3]

*gar* "to enclose, to assemble, to group"
*g'ar* (har) " " "

There is still in Sumerian,

*kar* "wall"[4]
*ingar* "ramparts, wall."

Besides we know that the vowel changes of the type of *a* : : *u* are frequent in Sumerian and the root *gar* can be found under the forms: [5]

[1] *Un ancien peuple du Penjab : les Udumbara in Journ. As.*, 1926, p. 7.

[2] Nevertheless it is possible that in some of these names, the element *-agara* represents Skt. *āgāra*.

[3] *Cf.* C. Autran, *Sumérien et Indo-Européen*, p. 82, and Delitsch, *Sumerisches Glossar*.

[4] Fr. Delitsch, *Glossar*, and C. Autran *Sumérien et Indo-Européen*, p. 82.

[5] Autran, *ibid*, p. 113.

*gar*—
*kar*— "to connect, to assemble"
*kur*

The Austro-Asiatic "verbal root" *kar, kur,* is found again in Sumerian with the same variations and semantic value.

On the other hand in Sumerian we also find:

*uru* "to found"
"habitation, city,"

a form which is sometimes reduced to *ur.*[1]

It is not improbable that the Sumerian series *kar, kur, uru, ur* contains some distinct roots of similar forms with similar meanings.

Nothing however permits us to decide definitely if the Indian series *kūra, *gūra, ūra, ūr,* with their variants *kara, *gara* is properly Austro-Asiatic or Sumerian. The indecisive character of the question is not at all negligible because it raises a new problem—that of the relation between Sumerian and Austro-Asiatic languages.

Mr. Autran has already pointed out [2] that *pan,* the Sumerian word for bow is analogous to the Austro-Asiatic words meaning "bow, to draw a bow." It may be said that this similarity is purely a fortuitous one. But with the Sumerian series *kar, kur, uru, ur* the uncertainty appears to be less. The examples of such similarity can be however multiplied. I shall content myself in pointing out the most suggestive ones:

| Sumerian. | Austro-Asiatic. |
|---|---|
| *g'a* "fish" | "fish" *ka* (common Austro-Asiatic). |

[1] Delitsch, *Glossar.*

[2] *Ibid*, p. 123, and *cf. B.S.L.*, XXV, pp. 56-59.

| Sumerian. | Austro-Asiatic. |
|---|---|
| *ku* " (*kúa*) " | |
| *sig* "skin covered with "hairs," | *sok* (Mon) |
| "hair," | *sok* (Stieng) |
| "wool" | *suk* (Old Khmer) |
| | *sog*, *suk*, *sak* } (Malay Peninsula) |
| *gàlu* "man" | "man" *kol* (common Munda) |
| | *kur* (Malày Peninsula) |
| *mulu* ,, | *mönö* (Halang) |
| *ur* ,, | *benü* (Lave) |
| | *ur-aṅ* (Čam) |
| | *oṛ-aṅ* (Malay) |
| *buru* "fruit" | "fruit" *pèli* |
| | *pèlè* (Malay Peninsula) |
| | *plē* |
| | *plei* (Bahnar) |
| | *phlé* (Khmer) |
| *gula* "great" | "great" *karū* |
| *gal* ,, | *kadū* (Nikobarese) |
| | *karū* (Chowra) |
| | *kadui* (Malay Peninsula) |
| *mah* "great" | Augmentative prefix *ma* |
| *nē̂* demonstrative | Demonstrative *ni*, *nē* (common Austro-Asiatic). |

These analogies, of which the list is not exhausted, can be explained as loan-words. It is neither impossible that Sumerian should be related to the Austric languages. But it would be premature to try to choose between the two alternatives.

# III

# Non-Aryan Loans in Indo-Aryan

## *Kodumbara, Odumbara*[1]

In a series of articles published in the *Mémoires* and the *Bulletin de la Société de Linguistique* I have begun to show, since 1920, what the Indo-Aryan vocabulary owes to the Austro-Asiatic[2] languages. After having prepared the way, I have marked out in these languages a certain number of words of which the initial has either

[1] Taken from Prof. J. Przyluski's article: *Un ancien peuple du Penjab : Les Udumbara*, *J. As.*, 1926, pp. 25-36.

[2] While speaking of "Austro-Asiatic" languages I attribute to this word a meaning of comprehensive nature not in use till now. I use it for designating a linguistic family which singularly surpasses the limits of Austric Asia. It is difficult to find a geographical term which will be sufficiently general to include all the languages spoken, not only in Eastern Asia but also in a large part of Oceania, Africa (Madagascar) and no doubt to the north of the Pacific in ancient times. "Austro-Asiatic" is suggested by the hypothesis that Austric Asia is the region whence the people speaking these languages seem to have dispersed. Such was the opinion of H. Kern who admitted the continental origin of the Malayo-Polynesian peoples. This hypothesis has not yet been confirmed by any fact. P. Schmidt who was the first to speak of "Austro-Asiatic" languages reserve this word for the languages of the continent and makes the "Austro-Asiatic" language a subdivision of the Austric language. This last term has the disadvantage of apparently confining the language, still largely spread to the north of the equator, only to the Austric hemisphere. Probably it would be better to reserve the word "Austric" for designating the languages spoken in Oceania before the arrival of the Malayo-Polynesians.

softened or completely disappeared. It is thus that for "son, child" we have the following forms :

*kon* *khon* *hān*[1]

In *hān* the guttural initial is reduced to an aspirate.

On the other hand in Khmer *ambas* "cotton" comes from an ancient **kambas* of which the guttural initial has completely disappeared (*Bulletin de la Société de Linguistique*, 1924, p. 70, and *supra*, p. 23). The comparison of the words for man and woman in the Munda languages reveals an analogous phenomenon :

| | | | | |
|---|---|---|---|---|
| "man" | *koro,* | *haṛ, hörŏl,* | *haṛa,* | *hoṛ* |
| "woman" | | *kūṛī,* | *koṛi,* | *ērā* |

Here for the same root we have different conditions of the initial, *k*, *h* and zero. It would be easy to show that the same phenomenon has occurred in the case of other initials in that linguistic family. Thus for "salt" we have :

*tampoying,* *empoya,* *ambang*[2]

For the "breast," Cam has two forms : *baraum̃* and *araum̃*. In Santali the *Hibiscus sabdariffa* is either *bambara* or *ambaro*. To *brang* "black" in Bahnar (<**berang*) corresponds *keram* in the speeches of the Malay Peninsula, *kireng* in Kawi and *ireng* in Javanese. It will be easy to multiply examples. When the principle once comes to light the difficulties begin in our attempt to draw conclusions from it.

[1] *Memoires de la Société de Linguistique*, 1921, p. 209 (*cf. supra*, p. 29). The form *hān* is common to several Munda languages : Mundari, Santali, etc.

[2] *Cf.* Skeat and Blagden : *Pagan Races of the Malay Peninsula*, II, p. 702.

Kusinārā is the Sanskrit name of a town which became famous by the *parinirvāṇa* of Buddha; the *Mahābhārata* (VIII, 5, v. 137; XII, 101, v. 3736) speaks of a people called Uśinara. These names form a pair of which the elements can be nearly superposed; the most notable difference is due to the loss of the initial in the second, a phenomenon frequent in the Austro-Asiatic languages. Can we deduce from it that the pair has been borrowed from that family of languages? It will be however imprudent. The apheresis is observed in different linguistic families. Sumerian (Autran, *Langues du Monde*, p. 278) furnishes some such examples and some Sanskrit words are precisely suspected to be loans from that language.

Even supposing that Sumerian has nothing to do here and that amongst the languages which were in contact with Indo-Aryan in ancient times those which belonged to the Austro-Asiatic family were the sole to present cases of aphereses, it would be still imprudent to say that the words which have lost their initial in Sanskrit would necessarily be of Austro-Asiatic origin. The softening of the initial $k > h$ appears to be due to the fact that, in the dialects in which it is produced the pronunciation of the occlusive necessitated a strong breath. The same pronunciation has been able to maintain itself and produce the same effects even after the non-Aryan populations of India had learnt to speak the Indo-Aryan languages and, since then, some words of Indo-European origin could have lost their initial.

In short, the loss of initial in some words of Indian languages would not prove their Austro-Asiatic origin. I cannot therefore admit without reservation the following formula in which Prof. Sylvain Lévi recently summarised the results of his researches on some Indian geographical names: "Pulinda-Kulinda, Mekala-Utkala (with the group Uḍra-Puṇḍra-Muṇḍa), Kosala-Tosala, Aṅga-Vaṅga, Kaliṅga-Tiliṅga form the links of a long chain which extends from the eastern confines of Kashmir up to the centre of the peninsula. The skeleton of this ethnical system is constituted by the heights of the central plateau; it participates in the life of all the great rivers of India, except the Indus in the west and the Kaveri in the south. Each of these groups form a binary whole; each of these binary units is united with another member of the system. In each ethnic pair the twin bears the same name, differentiated only by the initial: *k* and *t*; *k* and *p*; zero and *v* or *m* or *p*. This process of formation is foreign to Indo-European; it is foreign to Dravidian; it is on the contrary characteristic of the vast family of languages which are called Austro-Asiatic, and which covers in India the group of the Muṇḍā languages, often called also the Kolarian." (*Pré-aryen et pré-dravidien...*, *J. As.*, 1923, p. 30; *supra*, p. 95).

The difference between Aṅga and Vaṅga or Uḍra and Puṇḍra is not at all similar to that which exists between Pulinda and Kulinda, Kosala and Tosala. There is no reason to suppose that there is "the same process of formation" in all these cases. In the group Vaṅga-Aṅga, there is, I think, the same word which has either lost or preserved its initial and aphereses which is a purely phonetic phenomenon does not teach us anything certain on the origin of either Vaṅga or Aṅga. The same thing can be said about the group Uḍra-Puṇḍra-Muṇḍa, if we admit that these words can be rightly connected with each other. On the other hand the groups Pulinda-Kulinda, Kosala-Tosala differ by the permutation of two prefixes *pu* and *ku*, *ko* and *to* and this phenomenon, which is of morphological character, tends to prove the Austro-Asiatic origin of the words in which it is observed.

It is now clear that this discussion of principle was necessary before examining the significance of the group *Kodumbara-Odumbara*. We now know that the presence or absence of the initial *k* does not prove that the names are Austro-Asiatic. Before proceeding further it will be of advantage to discuss a second problem closely related to the first.

*A priori* nothing forbids us to say: Kulinda = K + ulinda; if I have abandoned that method of arguing it is because the Austro-Asiatic languages present derivatives of the type Ku-linda. *Ka* is a prefix frequently met with in these languages and the vowel *u* normally replaces there *a*. This indicates the way which we should follow. If *Kodumbara-Odumbara* form a pair in Middle-Indian and *Udumbara* in Sanskrit corresponds with them, we should start from the form **Kudumbara*.[1] Isolating the prefix *ku-* we should see if the element *dumbara* can-be explained in such a group of Non-Aryan languages. In short we have got to see if **kudumbara* can be normally derived from an Austro-Asiatic root by prefixing *ku-*.

The Indian flora possess a sort of coloquintida which the Botanists call *Lagenaria vulgaris* and which like a large number of gourds are of Eastern Asiatic origin. In Sanskrit the name of the fruit is *tumbā*; we have also *tumbī* and *tumbuka*. It is not at all possible to separate it from the word *goḍumba* which is used for

[1] As Prk. *odumbara* is derived from Skt. *udumbara* so also it is probable that Pali *kodumbara* comes from **kudumbara*.

water melon as well as for a kind of cucumber. *Goḍumba* certainly belongs to the same family as *tumbă*; the connection between these two words can be explained by the similarity of the two fruits.

We know on the other hand that several Austro-Asiatic people call themselves issue either of a gourd or a melon of which every seed gave birth to a man.[1] The same myth has passed into the Indian tradition. The wife of Sagara, king of Ayodhyā, named Sumati to whom 60,000 sons were promised, gave birth to a gourd from which 60,000 children came out. (*Rāmāy.* I, 38; *cf. Mahābhārata* III, 106; *Bhāgav. Pur.* IX, 8, 8). *Ikṣvāku*, the Sanskrit word for gourd is also the name of an ancestor of the kings of Ayodhyā. The Austro-Asiatic myth of gourd-ancestor has evidently been transposed in the legends of Sumati and Ikṣvāku, both of whom are placed at Ayodhyā. But as it often happens in Indian literature, it seems that in the second case, the authors have modified the myth for ennobling it. The epic poets could not be pleased by the fact that a gourd had given birth to a glorious dynasty. Ikṣvāku, which properly means a gourd, has been personified as a hero, son of Manu-Vaivasvata (*Rāmāy.* I, 70, v. 20-21; *Mahābhār.* I, 75, v. 3140), or that of ṛṣi Gautama (*cf.* Rockhill, *Life of the Buddha*, pp. 10-11). In a story of the *Dul-va* analysed by Rockhill, attempt has been made to explain the name of Ikṣvāku by the fact that the children of *ṛṣi* Gautama had been found in a field of sugarcane (*ikṣu*). This play on words should not deceive us; the difference between the epic and the

1 Bonifacy; *Cours d'ethnographie indo-chinoise*, Hanoi, 1919, p. 45; and Cochrane, *The Shans*, Rangoon, 1915, I, p. 120.

Buddhist traditions relating to Ikṣvāku shows how far the one or the other deviates from popular belief.

As *tumbā* is the name of a coloquintida and as, in the common traditions of India and Indo-China, the ancestor of a family or a tribe can be a gourd, there is nothing strange in the fact that the *Mahābhārata* knows the Tumbuma or Tumbura. This is the name of a people, apparently derived from *tumba* by affixing *ra* or *ma* of which the first is particularly frequent in the Indo-Aryan names. As regards the affix *ma*, I have shown elsewhere [1] that it is prefixed to some Indo-Aryan loan words borrowed from the Austro-Asiatic languages.

If we had altogether ignored the Pre-Aryan languages we could have supposed that *kudumbara* is a loan word in those languages and is derived from the word for gourd. But our information is not limited to Sanskrit. In Malay, *labu* means a gourd, and other cucurbits (*e. g.*, *labu merah* "*Cucurbita moschata*".) The corresponding forms are:

| | | | |
|---|---|---|---|
| Malay Peninsula | ... | ... | *labu, labo* |
| Khmer | ... | ... | *lbow* |
| Batak | ... | ... | *tabu* |
| Malagashy | ... | ... | *tavu* |

On the other hand in Sanskrit we have: *lābu, alābu, ālābū* (*cf.* Pali *lāpu, alāpu*) "*Lagenaria vulgaris*—gourd." The unsettled character of these forms is a sufficient indication of their non-Aryan origin. The comparison with Malay, Khmer, etc., confirms that these words have been borrowed from the Austro-Asiatic languages.

[1] *Bull. Soc. Ling.*, t. XXVI, p. 98 suiv.; *suppra*, pp. 129-135.

As the Indo-Aryan words for the *Lagenaria vulgaris* are of the type *tumba*, *labu* it is sufficiently significant that we have in the east: Batak *tabu*, Malay *labu*. It seems that in these two insular and continental regions the initial *l* permutes with *t*. One is therefore tempted to suggest as the origin of all these forms, an Austro-Asiatic form like **ṭumba* with a cerebral initial. The Austro-Asiatic languages really possessed and still possess a series of cerebrals—a fact which is of certain importance for the study of Indo-Aryan languages. Whatever role we may attribute to substratum in the development of cerebralisation in Indo-Aryan, the existence of a series of cerebrals in the Austro-Asiatic languages is a fact which nobody will be able to ignore.

The cerebral, however, appears in Sanskrit *goḍumba* "cucumber." This word can be easily explained by starting from an ancient **ṭumba*, by adding a prefix with a guttural initial and by converting the intervocalic *ṭ* [1] into a sonant. In the Indonesian languages the words for cucumber (*Cucumis sativus*) are comparable:

| | |
|---|---|
| Javanese, Malay, Sunda ... ... | *timun* |
| Javanese, Malay ... ... | *katimun* |
| Madura ... ... ... | *antemon* |

The root from which *tumba*, etc., are derived occurs again in *timun* in which the first vowel has changed its stem and thus *mb*>*m*. The prefix with guttural initial in

The cerebral of **tumba* which has disappeared in Sanskrit from the beginning of the word *tumba* is preserved in the interior of the word *goḍumba*. Similarly in some Austro-Asiatic languages, for example in Annamese, the old initial *ṭ* has become *t* while it is retained at the end of the word. It should be remarked that in Sanskrit there are very few words with cerebral initial.

*goḍumba* is found again in *ka-ti-mun,* and with apheresis in *antemon* (< **kantemon*). The initial *a* of Sanskrit *alābu* is probably also the rest of an ancient prefix.

In Javanese *walu* is the form which corresponds to Malay *labu*; *walu,* without doubt, comes from **luwa* (<**ṭumba*) by metathesis. Several other Indo-Chinese words for gourd can be connected with the latter: Bahnar *puol*; Rongao *pŭöl*; Kha *păr* and similarly Annamese *bằ'u* "*Lagenaria vulgaris,* gourd."

We now see how many different forms the same root has taken in the vast domain where it has spread. It is little probable that these variations are solely due to the normal display of phonetic laws. We know that the words having religious import are subject to systematic deformation; the word being tabooed under its normal form, was much changed in use. The myth of gourd-mother sufficiently explains the respectful fear, inspired by the name of this fruit and the modifications the word has undergone.

On the whole, it seems that an Austro-Asiatic root like **ṭumba,* either accompanied by affixes or not, has been used to mean the cucurbit, *i.e.,* the fruit which contains a large number of seeds in it. To the same family belongs the Sanskrit loan words: *tumbā, tumbī, tumbuka, goḍumba, lābu, alābu, ālābū.* The same root explains still a few other Indo-Aryan words.

*Udumbara* is the Sanskrit word for *Ficus glomerata,* a tree which is native of Burma and found in India principally in the Sub-Himalayan zone (Watt, *Dictionary of conomic Products of India,* s. v°. *Ficus glomerata*). The fruit of this tree resembles the European fig except that it is smaller and of oval shape. Its shape is rightly comparable to that of some small coloquintidas and the large number of seeds which it contains adds to the resemblance.[1] Therefore we need not be surprised to find an analogy between the names of the coloquintida: Sanskrit *tumbā*, and that of *Ficus glomerata*: Sanskrit *udumbara*. It may be remarked however that the cerebral of **ṭumba* reappears in the classical Sanskrit form *uḍumbara*. Sueh *rapprochements* seem to be more justified when we consider the very words for *udumbara* in the modern languages of India: Santali *lowa*; Chota Nagpur *dume*; Kherwarien *dumer*; Oriya *dimeri*; Nepal *dumri*. [Bengali *dumur*—P. C. B.]. Between *labu*, the Malay word for different kinds of gourds (the Sanskrit equivalent *lābu*, the corresponding word in Javanese *walu*) and *lowa* the word for *Ficus glomerata* in Santali, the resemblance is as exact as possible and can be very well explained by semantic laws.

What does then the initial *u* in Sanskrit *udumbara* represent? This cannot but be the rest of an ancient prefix which has now lost its initial and the analogy of *ketimun*, *goḍumba* suggests here an ancient guttural. *Udumbara* | *uḍumbara* then would come from an ancient **kutumbara* | **kuṭumbara* and we are thus brought back in a roundabout way to the hypothesis already formulated above.[2]

It is probably in the same family, from which Sanskrit *tumba*, *udumbara*, etc., come, that we have to search for the origin of names of some musical instruments and an Indian caste. *Lābukī*, the word for a sort of

[1] In the eyes of the Austro-Asiatics the abundance of seeds was certainly the characteristic feature of these fruits, as the myth of the gourd-mother giving birth to numerous children shows.

[2] Of the two kindred words for the cotton stuff in Pali the one has a cerebral: *koṭumbara* while the other has not got it: *kodumbara*.

lute is certainly derived from Skr. *lābu* "gourd."[1] *Ḍamaru* is the Sanskrit and the Bengali name of a small drum which plays an important role in Indian iconography as the attribute of several divinities (*cf.* Curt Sachs, *Die Musikinstrumente Indiens und Indonesiens*, 2nd ed., p. 75). The instrument called in Marathi *ḍámru*, in Hindi *ḍamrū*, etc., resembles a gourd, with two swellings, cut in such a way as to have only the two hemispheric ends. The analogy of the names of this drum with those of the *udumbara* fruit in the Indian languages can be therefore explained by their common ressemblance to some cucurbits. *Tamburā* is the Marathi word for a kind of *vīṇā*. It does not appear doubtful at all that the instrument owes its name to that of the two hollow appendices which are suspended from the tube like the gourds from their stalk.[2]

[1] *Cf.* also the name of a kind of Bengali violin: *alābu sārangī* (Curt Sachs, p. 131).

[2] This cithara must not be confounded with a lute which has almost the same name: Hindi *ṭamburā* (Curt Sachs, *ibid*, p. 129, fig. 90), but which resembles a mandolin of which the body is like a big calabash. Mr. C. Sachs is of opinion that the name of this instrument is the same as Persian *ṭanbur*, which is derived by metathesis from *pandur*, name of a lute in the Near East. India would have received the *ṭanbūr* from her western neighbours and modified the name by analogy to that of Tumburu, the king of celestial musicians. In fact it seems that Hindi *ṭamburā* designates an instrument imported to India from the west but it is difficult to decide if the Hindi form *ṭamburā* is due to a contamination with the name of Tumburu or that of the cithara called *ṭamburā* in Marathi. This last instrument seems to be indigenous in India and its name can be explained by the two calabashes hanging from it. It is not however impossible that Tumburu owes its name originally to the musical instrument which has the shape of a gourd or a calabash; according to this hypothesis the name of the *gandharva* king would also belong to the family: *tumba*, *udumbara*, etc.

Last of all, *ḍomba,* in Sanskrit, is the name of a low caste earning its livelihood by chanting and singing. The word appears under the form *Ḍomva* (*Ḍova*) in the list of the Mlecchas taken by Weber from the Jaina texts (*Indische studien,* XVI, p. 332). In the modern languages of India, *dome, dhombe, dombar, dombarī, dumbar, dumbaru* designate the degraded aborigines scattered all over India (*Hobson-Jobson,* s. v. *dombe*). It seems that the same non-Aryan word or its variants have been used for the musical instruments made of gourd or calabash, as well as for the native musicians who played on that instrument and the caste from which these poor musicians were recruited.

On the whole, *udumbara,* the Sanskrit word for *Ficus glomerata,* belongs to the long series of words borrowed by the Indo-Aryan languages from the Austro-Asiatic ones. Udumbara also designates a country of the Penjab and its inhabitants. It has been observed that in the neighbouring countries in the South-Sea, the names of peoples or countries are frequently borrowed from the vegetable world. If the name *udumbara* is of Austro-Asiatic origin, there is nothing surprising that the name of a people and a country has been derived from this tree. On the other hand, the economic and linguistic history forbids us to separate from it the word *kodumbara,* which is used for a sort of tissue as well as for the people who used to make it. It should therefore be admitted that Udumbara, Odumbara, Kodumbara are the variants of the same name of an Austro-Asiatic people of Northern India.

# APPENDIX

## TO

## PART III

# I

## Paloura-Dantapura[1]

( Sylvain Le'vi )

On the eastern coast of India Ptolemy mentions a locality called Paloura (VII, 1, 16) which he chooses as one of the bases for the preparation of his map. He places Paloura at 136° 40′ East × 11° 20′ North at the entrance of the Gangetic gulf and at 20′ North of the *apheterium* where the vessels bound for the "Peninsula of Gold" (Khrusê Khersonêsos) ceased to follow the littoral and entered the high sea. The map of Ptolemy places the *apheterium* at the southern extremity of an imaginary peninsula which inclines south-eastwards starting from a point which approximately agrees with the Calimere point, right to the north of Ceylon and passes straight to the north for extending at last in the west-east direction towards the Gangetic delta. In his first book (I, 13, 5-7) Ptolemy had already discussed in detail the position attributed to Paloura by his predecessor, the navigator of Tyr, and corrected in his own way the distance indicated by this navigator between Paloura and the port of Sada, on the opposite coast.

One is surprised to find that a locality placed in such an exceptional situation on the route of maritime commerce between India and the Far-East, is not mentioned elsewhere. The name belongs to the Dravidian type ; it is one

[1] *Cf. J. As.*, 1925 pp. 46-57 (*Notes Indiennes*) already referred to by Prof. Przyluski ; *cf. supra*, p. 136.

of the long series of names ending in **our* and **oura*, an element which has long been recognised as the Dravidian word *ūr* "city." Caldwell (*Comp. Grammar of the Dravidian Languages*, Introd., p. 104) has explained the name Paloura by Tamil *pāl-ūr* "the city of milk." But another explanation can also be offered. In Tamil for 'tooth' we have the word *pallu* (Telugu : *pallu* ; Canarese : *hallu* ; Malayalam : *pallu* ; Gond : *pal*, etc. ; cf. *Linguistic Survey*, Vol. IV, 650-652, No. 37) ; Paloura can be the "city of tooth." The Indian tradition is acquainted and since long, with a "city of tooth," Dantapura, in the country of Kaliṅga, just in the same region in which Paloura is located. It is only in the Buddhist tradition that Dantapura has become famous ; the name of the town is associated there with a famous relic, the tooth of Buddha, which is worshipped till to-day at Kandy in Ceylon. The common tradition on the division of the relics just after the *Parinirvāṇa* relates that one of the teeth of the Master passed to the kingdom of Kaliṅga (Dīgha, II, p. 167 ; Buddhavaṁsa, Chap. XXVIII ; *Dulva* in Rockhill, *Life*, p. 147). A late poem in Pali, the *Dāṭhāvaṁsa* (ed. J. P. T. S. 1884) by Dhammakitti, relates the pretended history of this relic ; it was brought to Dantapura by the Muni Khema, under the reign of Kāliṅga Brahmadatta ; it remained there as the object of a cult till the reign of Guhasīva who for saving it from defilement, entrusted it to his son-in-law, Dantakumāra of Ujjayinī ; it was taken by him to Tāmralipti, and thence on board a vessel to Ceylon where it was piously received by the successor of Mahāsena, Kitti-siri-megha (middle of the 4th century A.D.), the same prince who had sent an envoy to Samudragupta for the Mahābodhi monastery. The two facts are related to each other; Kitti-siri-megha seems to have imposed himself as a champion of Buddhist interests at a time when India was passing through a period of reaction against that religion.

For the Buddhist tradition, Dantapura is one of the most ancient cities of India; it appears as the first in the list of six cities built by Mahā Govinda, in the time of King Reṇu:

> Dantapuraṁ Kāliṅgānaṁ Assakānañ ca Potanaṁ
> Māhissatī Avantīnaṁ Sovīrānañ ca Rorukaṁ
> Mithilā ca Videhānaṁ Campā Aṅgesu māpitā
> Bārāṇasī ca Kāsīnaṁ ete Govindamāpitā.

This versified list has been inserted in the Mahā Govinda Sutta of the Dīgha Nikāya, XIX, 36; it is also found in the corresponding Sūtra of the Dīrghāgama, extant in two Chinese versions, the one (Tōk; XII, 9, 28ᵃ, 5) incorporated in the *Chang A-han*—the long Āgama and the other translated separately (XII, 10, 50ᵃ, 3) by She-hu (Dānapāla). It also occurs in the Mahāvastu, III, 208. Several stories of the Mahāvastu have for their scene Dantapura in the country of the Kaliṅga, III, 361, 364 (similarly *cf.* also the Pāli Jātaka: *Kurudhamma* II, 67; *Culla Kaliṅga*, III, 3; *Kumbhakāra*, II, 376; *Kaliṅgabodhi* IV, 230); they likewise speak of events which took place "at the time when Kāliṅga was reigning at Dantapura in Kaliṅga" (*Kaliṅgaraṭṭhe Dantapuranagare Kāliṅge rajjaṁ kārente*). In the *Kumbhakāra (jātaka)* the king who reigns at Dantapura in Kaliṅga is the famous Karaṇḍu, whose name is associated with those of Naggaji of Gandhāra, Dummukha of Uttara-Pañcala, and Nimi of Videha who abdicated for living like ascetics. Their glory is not less in the Jaina literature where Karaṇḍu is transformed into Karakaṇḍu, who was also king of Kaliṅga at Dantapura; the magnificent Jaina encyclopaedia, now in course of publication, the Abhidhāna-Rājendra, relates at length the biography of Karakaṇḍu (s.v.°) and refers to a series of texts; it will suffice here to retain the account of the *Uttarādhyāyana sūtra*, XVIII, 45-46, with the commentary of Devendra. Dantapura of Kaliṅga is also famous amongst the Jainas as the capital of King Dantavakra (°vakka), "the best of the Kṣatriyas" according to the *Sūtrakṛtāṅga* I, 6, 22, specially known for having involuntarily roused an emulation of devotion and heroism between two friends, Dhanamitra and Dṛḍhamitra, the Indian parallel of Orestes and Pylades or of Damon and Pythias, etc.; the word *danta* "tooth" or "tusk" has suggested the beginning of the story: the wife of King Dantavakra, who was *enceinte* had a desire; she wanted a palace entirely built of ivory; the king therefore orders to keep all available ivory reserved for his use. Unfortunately, the wife of the merchant Dhanamitra, who was also *enceinte*, was seized by the same desire; for satisfying her the merchant and his friend do not obey the order of the king; then each of them puts forth his claim to be punished; the king is moved and pardons them (*cf.* Abhidhāna-Rājendra s.v.° *pacchitta*, Vol. V, p. 186, and for the references s.v.° Dantavakka).

The Mahā-Bhārata mentions a prince named Dantavakra (*pass.*; *cf.* Sorensen, *Index*, s.v.°) but he is the king of Kārūṣa, the country situated between Cedi and Magadha, to the south of Kāśi and Vatsa. Dantavakra, the Kārūṣa, is mentioned quite frequently in the Harivaṁśa, almost always in the company of Kaliṅga; he is the terrible adversary of Kṛṣṇa who at last kills him.

That is doubtless the origin of the reading adopted by the Southern manuscripts, in the passage of the Mahā-Bhārata quoted later on (p. 168): "He (Kṛṣṇa) has destroyed the Kaliṅga [and] Dantavaktra."

I have not been able to discover any reference to Dantapura in the Brahmanical literature; however a late epigraphic evidence proves that the name of this locality was in use for a long time. King Indravarman issues a donation from his residence at Dantapura (*Dantapuravāsakāt*; *Ep. Ind.*, XIV, 361 : Purle Plates of Indravarman, the [Gaṅga] year 149) while the kings of this dynasty generally issue their charts from Kaliṅganagara. Indravarman makes to a Brahmin the donation of the village of Bhukkukūra, in the Kūraka-rāṣṭra (modern Bhukkur in the Pālakoṇḍa Tāluk), the place where the inscription was found. The editor of the inscription, G. Ramadas, observes : "On the road from Chicacole to Siddhāntam [the name of a village which Mr. Ramadas wants to reconstruct as Siddhārthaka-grāma—'the village of the Buddhists'! ] and very near this last place a large piece of land is shown as the site of the fort of Dantavaktra." Mr. Ramadas, if he had known the Jaina legends, would not have missed to notice the really surprising persistence of the memory of King Dantavaktra or Dantavakra (the forms alternate and are confounded with each other in Prākrit Danta-vakka) about whom the legend connected with the name of Dantapura has been just now mentioned.

Though the Mahā-Bhārata does not contain any mention of Dantapura yet it refers, on several occasions in connection with Kaliṅga, to a name of which the first element is *danta*. In the 5th canto (*adhy*. 23, v. 708), Yudhiṣṭhira, while recalling the exploits of his brothers speaks out,

"The son of Mādrī, Sahadeva, has vanquished the Kaliṅgas assembled at Dantakūra by throwing lance right and left!"—

Mādrīputraḥ Sahadevaḥ Kaliṅgān samāgatān ajayad Dantakūre | Vāmenāsyan dakṣiṇenaiva yo vai mahābalaṁ kaccid enaṁ smaranti ||

Further on in the same canto when Saṁjaya reports the words of Arjuna glorifying Kṛṣṇa (*adhy*. 47, v. 1883): "It is he who has vanquished the Pāṇḍya at Kavāṭa and destroyed the Kaliṅgas at Dantakūra."

ayaṁ Kavāṭe nijaghāna Pāṇḍyaṁ
tathā Kaliṅgān Dantakūre mamarda |

Against this passage the translation of P. C. Roy has: "It was he who slew King Pāṇḍya by striking his breast against his and mowed down the Kaliṅgas in battle." The translator adds in a note "some texts read *kapāṭe nijaghāna* meaning 'slew in the city of Kapāṭa.'" For his translation he has followed the reading of the Calcutta edition: *kapāṭena jaghāna*. The meaning, as is evident, is quite different. The translator has followed the commentary of Nīlakaṇṭha, who adopts *kapāṭena jaghāna* and interprets *kapāṭa* as "thorax, the breast as large as the door-piece;" Nīlakaṇṭha, in the second *pāda*, arbitrarily attributes the meaning of "the battle in which one shows the teeth" to the word *dantakūra*.

The southern edition reads (*adhy*. 48, v. 76) *kavāṭe nijaghāna* and *dantavaktraṁ mamarda*. The gloss interprets *kavāṭe* as *nagarabheda* "a particular town;" it is silent about the rest. It is however curious to see the King Dantavaktra, persistently associated with Kaliṅga, reappearing here, even in defiance of the syntax which does not allow two accusatives juxtaposed (*tathā kaliṅgān dantavaktrāṁ mamarda*).

The word *dantakūra* is again mentioned in the Mahā-Bhārata, VII, 70, 7 at least in the Southern edition. The poet recalls the exploits of Paraśurāma in his fierce fight against the Kṣatriyas. "There, fourteen thousand enemies of the Brāhmaṇas and others still, he stopped them and killed them at Dantakūra."

*Brahmadviṣāṁ cātha tasmin sahasrāṇi caturdaśa*
*punaranyān nijagrāha Dantakūre jaghāna ha.*

The commentator mentions another reading, *danta-krūram*; "in this case, he says, the word designates the king of the country." To say in other words, when it is not a place-name formed with **kūra*, it is the name of a man formed with **krūra* "cruel;" and one should take it in the accusative. The translation of P. C. Roy follows the reading *Dantakūre* and translates the passage thus: "In that slaughter were included fourteen thousand Brāhmaṇa-hating Kshattriyas of the Dantakūra country." The Calcutta edition has preferred to read *Dantakrūraṁ jaghāna ha*; it is also the reading followed by Nīlakaṇṭha whose gloss (*taddeśā-dhipati*) has been reproduced by the annotator of the Southern edition. The authors of the Petersburg Dictionary have (s. v.° *dantakrūram*) treated the word as an adverb and translated it as "auf eine grauenvolle Weise mit den Zähnen" = "in a ferocious way with the teeth;" they have referred to this passage only. But later on, in the abridged edition, Böhtlingk substitutes the nominal stem *dantakrūra* for the adverb *dantakrūram* and interprets it thus: "Name of place (according to Nīlakaṇṭha); it should be read as *dantakūre* instead of *dantakrūram*."

The choice between *Dantakūra* and *Dantakrūra*, left uncertain by the tradition of the Mahā-Bhārata and the meaning of the word too, also uncertain, are definitely fixed by the evidence of Pliny. In Book VI, xx, he proposes to give the measurement of the coast up to the Indus, as he finds it, by indicating the distances, though there is no agreement amongst the different itineraries. He indicates as the first step : *ab oslio Gangis ad promontorium Calingōn et oppidum Dandagula DCXXV M. passuum* : "From the mouth of the Ganges to the promontory of Calinga and the fortified place of Dandagula, 625,000 steps." The promontory of Calinga, which constitutes so clear a starting point for measuring the coast, is evidently, without any doubt, the point where Ptolemy locates the *apheterium* of navigation towards the peninsula of Gold and which marks according to him a sudden change in the direction of the littoral. The nearest *oppidum* cannot be anything except Paloura of Ptolemy, otherwise called Dantapura and in the spelling of Pliny : Dandagula ; it is easy to recognise in it the name of Dantakura The distance of 625,000 steps, retained by Pliny from the confused data of the itineraries, correspond to 3,645 stadia. Ptolemy calculates 500 stadia for one degree to the equator and consequently on each meridian ; the distance from the Ganges to Dandagula would therefore correspond to about 6° 36′ in Ptolemy. Between Paloura and the westernmost mouth of the Ganges Ptolemy indicates a distance of 7° 50′ in longitude (136° 40′—144° 30′) and 6° 55′ in lattitude (11° 20′—18° 15′). It appears therefore that Ptolemy worked on data which were very near the approximate calculation of Pliny : but for the conception of the whole, which forced a systematic deformation, he would have arrived at a sufficiently faithful localisation in this part of his map ; the delta of the Ganges is placed towards 22° degree in the north; the region in which Dantapura can be conveniently searched for and where the local tradition still locates the fort (*oppidum*) of Dantavaktra is in the neighbourhood of Chicacole and Kaliṅgapatam, "the city of the Kaliṅgas," a little to the north of 18° degree; the distance between these two points is of 5 to 6 degrees along the littoral.

I have shown elsewhere [1] that the *aphetērion eis Khrusēn* of Ptolemy is identical with Caritrapura of Hiuan tsang and some Sanskrit texts. I would point out another feature more common both to the Greek and the Chinese. Ptolemy, as we have seen, places the *apheterium* at a promontory where the coast turns suddenly from the direction of W. N. W.-E. S. E., to that of S.-N., inclined at last towards the East separating the Argarique gulf from the Gangetic. The Caritrapura of Hiuan tsang is situated on the South-Eastern border of Orissa (*Mém.*, III, 90), and to the North-East of the kingdom of Malakuṭa (*ibid*, 124). Orissa, towards the South-East borders the kingdom of *Kong-yu-t'o*, Koṅgoda which formed a maṇḍala of Dakṣiṇakośala and corresponds to the present district of Ganjam. "The frontiers of this kingdom," writes Hiuan tsang, "embrace several tens of small towns which touch the hills and are situated at the confluence of two seas." Such is at least the translation of Julien; Watters (*Notes*, II, 197), criticises it and says, "there is no word for *two* in the text and the term *hai kiao* here means the meeting of sea and land." The pilgrim wished his readers to understand that the towns at one extremity 'continued the hills' (*kie shan*

[1] *Cf. Études Asiatiques* published by l'École Française d'Extrême Orient I.

*ling*) and at the other were on the sea shore. I would not enter into this Sinological discussion: I must however point out that the word *kiao* regularly means "meeting point; exchange, mixture," and the expression "situated at the meeting-point of seas" very well renders the geographical conception which Ptolemy had adopted for *apheterium*.

To find a well defined turning point along the eastern coast it is necessary to go up to the Palmyras Point which brings one to the mouths of the Ganges, at 20° 44′ 40″ N. × 87° 2′ E. to the north of the mouth of the Mahānadī. But Ptolemy places the *apheterium* right to the south of this river which he calls Manadas, midway between its mouth and the mouth of the Maisōlos which represents at the same time the Godāvarī and the Kistna. Besides, the current which, during the South-Western monsoon, passes from the Indian coast to that of Burma, avoids the Indian coast in the region of Chicacole at Kalingapatam at about 18° degree. I refer once again to the text of Valentijn (1727) which Yule has pointed out (*Proceed. Roy. Geogr. Soc.* 1882): "In the beginning of February, a small vessel sailed......towards Pegu with a cargo which she took at Masulipatam...... From this point she followed the coast up to the 18° degree north and thence she reached the high sea for attaining the opposite shore at 16° degree." The Maps of India, even in the 17th century, for example, that of William Blaca, continue to mark a sudden turn and inclination of the coast, in conformity with the indications of Ptolemy, between the ports of Masulipatam and Bimlipatam (to the north of Vizagapatam at 17° 53′ 15″ N. and 83° 29′ 50″ E.).

Moreover, it would be rather naive to wish to interprete the data of Ptolemy too literally for all this region;

the precision in his orders should not deceive anybody on the real worth of his knowledge. He locates Paloura a little to the north of the *apheterium* : Pliny, on the other hand, starting from the mouths of the Ganges, mentions first "the promontory of the Calingae" and then, consequently to its south, "the fortified place of Dandagula ;" Ptolemy ignores the name of Kalinga, either territorial or littoral ; perhaps one should recognise this name, still famous, in the city of Kalliga which Ptolemy LII. ¹. 93 enumerates amongst "the inland cities" of Maisōloi where Pitundra also is met with. I had already the occasion of pointing out the strange transposition by which he has taken Tosalī (Tōsalei mētropolis) of Orissa right into the territory of Pegu ; it seems that the whole of Orissa and a part of the neighbouring countries have undergone a similar transposition, probably through the confusion of the two itineraries, one inland from the South to the North and the other maritime from the West to the East.

Now that the name Dantakūra is well established as a geographical term, analogous to or identical with Dantapura, one will be surprised to recognise the enigmatic element *kūra* in the name of the kingdom Kūrakarāṣṭra ; the village Bhukkukūra, given by King Indravarman while he was at Dantapura, formed a part of the latter kingdom. The editor of the chart, Mr. Ramadas, is astonished to find here the term *rāṣṭra* "kingdom" while the provinces of Kaliṅga are elsewhere designated as *viṣaya*. The Kūraka or Kūra kingdom was perhaps an ancient expression, retained in a long use, for designating the territory near the capital Dantapura.

This singular element °*kūra* which appears to be alternating with Sanskrit °*pura* for designating in combination with *Danta*°, the capital of Kaliṅga, recalls, at least through analogy, the last syllable of the name of the city which Ptolemy writes Hippokoura (VII, 1, 83). Hippokoura is situated in the southern part of Ariakē to the south of Paithana (Paithan, in the upper valley of the Godavari, in the dominions of Nizam, district of Aurangabad) and Tagara (Ter, Ther, in the dominion of Nizam, district Naldrug), and to the north of Banaouasei (Banavasi in Mysore, district Shimoga). Hippokoura like Dantakūra, is a royal capital; it is *basileion Baleokourou*, "the royal residence of Baleokouros." The name of the sovereign also seems to reveal an element °*kūra*. Baleokouros is, without any doubt, an approximate transcription of the mysterious Viḷivāyakura, which is joined with the name of kings Sātakarṇi Vāsiṣṭhīputra and Sātakarṇi Gautamīputra, on a special type of coin, different from the type generally used by these two princes and confined only to the southern part of the Mahraṭha country, more precisely to the district of Kolhapur, which agrees well by its situation to the point which Ptolemy indicates for Hippokoura. On the title of Viḷivāyakura I cannot but repeat on my part what Prof. Rapson has said in his excellent *Catalogue of the Coins of the Andhra Dynasty*, 1908, to which I also refer for the description of the coins: "No satisfactory explanation has as yet been given of the forms *Vilivāyakura* and *Sivalakura*" (p. lxxxvii). "Sivalakura" which is coupled in the same way with the name of King Māḍharīputra, contains also the element °*kura*. The name of Hippokoura reappears in the Tables of Ptolemy (VII, 2, 6) as the name of a port situated in the immediate neighbourhood and a little to the south of Simulla (Cemula, Chaul, 23 miles south of Bombay); the Periplus does not mention it. Since this latter Hippokoura is located by Ptolemy on the littoral of Ariakē, which is distinguished as Ariakē Sadinōn, it may be asked if it is not the same locality, carried to the sea-shore through a wrong interpretation of the itineraries.

One may feel inclined to compare the final °*koura* in Hippokoura with °*kourai* which appears to be the plural form in the name of Sōsikourai (VII, 1, 10) which certainly corresponds to Tuticorin ; here *kourai* is doubtless the equivalent of the Tamil word *kuḍi* " place of habitation, town " (*cf.* the texts, s. v.° Tuticorin in Hobson-Jobson by Yule and Burnell). But the identity *kūra-kourai* is very doubtful.

Whatever might be the interpretation of the term *kūra*, the identity Paloura = Dantapura seems to be now definitely established. The geography of ancient India thus finds in Pliny and Ptolemy new data for localising the site of a large city of the past. The alternance Paloura-Dantapura, besides, shows that in the time of Ptolemy the Dravidian language was disputing the territory of Kaliṅga with the Aryan dialect. Even to our day, Chicacole and Kaliṅgapatam and the tāluk of Palkonda are in the Telegu country ; the limit between the Aryan and the Dravidian apparently is more to the north, almost midway between Chicacole and Ganjam (cf. *Linguistic Survey*, IV, 577).

# II

## Note on Tosala and Dhauli

(*Cf.* p. 71)[1]

*Text*[2] *of* Gaṇḍavyūha *quoted on p. 69.*

Gaccha kulaputrehaiva Dakṣiṇāpathe Amitatosale janapade Tosalaṁ nāma nagaraṁ tatra Sarvagāmī parivrājako prativasati......Yenāmitatosalo janapadas tenopajagāmopetya Tosalaṁ nagaraṁ parimārgan parigaveṣamāṇo 'nupūrveṇa Tosalaṁ nagaram anuprāptaḥ sūryāstaṁgamanakāle sa Tosalaṁ nāma nagaram anupraviśya madhye nagaraśṛṅgāṭakasya sthitvā vīthīmukhena vīthīmukhaṁ catvareṇa catvaraṁ rathyayā rathyāṁ Sarvagrāmiṇam adrākṣīt rātryāṁ praśāntāyāṁ Tosalasya nagarasyottare digbhāge Surabhaṁ nāma parvataṁ tasya śikhare vividhatṛṇagulma-auṣadhivanārāmaracite mahāvabhāsaprāptaṁ bhāskaram ivoditaṁ tasya tam avabhāsaṁ dṛṣṭvā......(MSS. 33, 36, 41 of the Bibliothèque Nationale de Paris).

This text of the *Gaṇḍavyūha* locates the mountain Surabha to the north of the city of Tosala; the Chinese translation of Buddhabhadra (398-421 A. D.) follows the text faithfully. But the translation of Śikṣānanda and Prājña differs and locates it to the east of the city. They

[1] I am glad to be able to add this note from the account furnished by my friend Mr. Nirmal Kumar Bose, M.A., who has travelled in this tract on many occasions in connection with anthropological studies.—P. C. B.

[2] This text is omitted on p. 69 through a mistake of mine.—P. C. B.

translated the official MS. of the King of Orissa—which should be considered as more authoritative in this case.

If Tosala is identified with Dhauli or its immediate neighbourhood then the mountain Surabha is to be identified with the Dhauli hill (also called Dhavalagiri) as it is the only hill in that tract. Dhauli is situated to the south or south-east of Bhuvaneswar at a distance of about 5 miles. The usual route to be followed is the metalled road from Bhuvaneswar to Puri. It passes by an ancient site known as Sisupalgarh and traverses the Dayānadi which is to be crossed by ferry. The Dhauli hill is situated to the west of this road, near the river. To the south-east of the Dhauli hill there is a large pool of water called Kausullā-gang, which is still fed by the Dayānadi during the rainy season when the water flows into it by a stretch of lowland to the north of the Dhauli hill. It was in all probability a dam, made from an old river-bed, in which water was preserved for the time of scarcity. There is still the mark of an embankment which stretched from the foot of the hill southwards along the Kausullā-gang. Admitting that the pool of water was an artificial dam, it must have been used to supply water to a neighbouring town which has now disappeared, and was situated by the side of the embankment. The boundaries of that town were probably the river on the west, the Kausullā-gang on the east and the Dhauli hill on the north or north-east. It is difficult to determine if the river has changed its course in recent times. But a study of the map shows that the main current now flows by the river Bargovi.

It should be pointed out that Asoka's inscription is found on the Eastern side of the Dhauli hill (facing the highroad from Bhuvaneswar to Puri). If this road, in ancient times, passed by the town we are trying to locate, it had probably taken a more easterly direction and passed by the side of the hill and the Kausullā-gang.

If ancient Tosali is located at the site indicated above then the Dhauli hill stood on its north or north-east, as the accounts of the *Gaṇḍavyūha* want us to believe, and the Kausullā-gang was to its east. The word *gang* is generally taken in the sense of river. *Kausullā-gang* therefore seems to have been originally a branch of the river. It may be suggested that *Kausullā* is most probably based on the word *Kosala*.

## ADDITIONS AND CORRECTIONS

| *page* | *line* | *for* | *read* |
|---|---|---|---|
| 35 | 18 | is ... ... | seems to be |
| 36 | 6-7 | the sources of information available | the present state of our knowledge |
| ,, | 21 | the movement ... | movements |
| ,, | 28 | (*J. As.*, 1923, I, p. 135) | (but see *J. As.*, 1923, I, p. 136) |
| 37 | 24 | a family ... | families |
| 38 | 18-20 | "If we ... northern side" | "we must look into northern Dravidian, if we wish to understand the history of southern languages" |
| ,, | 22 | certainly has been very recently acquired | is concerned only with their modern state |
| ,, | 26 | though it is ... | though, generally speaking, it is |
| 39 | 1 | 'in a general way' ... | to be omitted |
| ,, | 2-3 | Insert "it has happened" | before "through" |
| ,, | last line | cerebrla ... | cerebral |
| 41 | 23-24 | Omit "not only" and | "but goes farther back." |
| ,, | 30 | *Aika* ... ... | *aika* |
| 42 | 9 | very recent ... | 'comparatively recent' |
| 44 | 3 | (from bottom): "which is to be" | "which has been" |

| *page* | *line* | *for* | | *read* |
|---|---|---|---|---|
| 45 | 12 | "p. 199" | ... | "p. 179" |
| „ | 14 | "for the" | ... | "for an" |
| „ | 19 | "The only thing left is to consider" | | "So what remains to be compared are only" |
| „ | 23-25 | "To illustrate the course of a parallel evolution nothing more is necessary" | | "Nothing more is necessary to explain why in course of a parallel evolution ..." |
| „ | 25 | Omit "than to mention that" | | |
| 46 | 11 | "facts of a substratum" | | "facts due to a substratum" |
| 47 | 13 | *Kudirei* ... | ... | *kudirei* |
| „ | „ | *Kōṛā* ... | ... | *kōṛā* |
| „ | 16 | *Krutā* ... | ... | *krutā* |
| „ | 21 | *kui* ... | ... | kui |
| „ | 2 | (from bottom) : MSL XIX, p. 89 | | Ind. Ant. XLVIII, p. 195 |
| „ | last line | fouud ... | ... | found |
| „ | 17 | *Kuli* ... | ... | *kuli* |
| 50 | 5 | Add : "Further, in the absence of other proofs no borrowing from Dravidian will be admitted for Indo-Aryan words with aspirates." | | |
| „ | 21 | *kalte* ... | ... | *kalte.* |
| „ | 23 | Add : (*cf. Jules Bloch —Le nom du Riz : E'tudes Asiatiques*) | | |

| *page* | *line* | *for* | *read* |
|---|---|---|---|
| 51 | 2 | *bōkā* ... ... | *varkār* |
| „ | 8 | *Ernout* ... ... | Ernout |
| „ n. 1, | 5 | *Tibetan Loan Words* ... | *Loan Words in Tibetan* |
| 52 | 22 | *melasu* ... ... | *meṇasu* |
| 53 | 18 | *viçu* ... ... | *vīçu* |
| „ | „ | *vivu* ... ... | *vīvu* |
| „ | 3 | (from bottom) : *mali* | *namali* |
| 54 | 20 | *panjnā* ... ... | *panjkā* |
| „ | „ | Add after "fruit" ... | Gon. *paṇḍnā*, Kur. *panjnā* "to ripen." |
| 55 | 3 | "ordinary article" ... | "article of ordinary use" |
| „ | 21-22 | which the Afghan has borrowed | which is found only in Afghan |
| 56 | 4 | (from bottom) : *oth* ... | *oṭh* |
| 57 | 4 | "for it" ... | "for words with aspirates" |
| „ | 12 | *misī* ... ... | *mīsi* |
| „ | 13 | *miçei* ... ... | *mīçei* |
| „ | 16 | Przylaski ... | Przyluski |
| „ | 17 | *cramuh* ... | *čramuh* |
| „ n. 1, | 6 | "*façade* in the back" | "the courtyard in the backside of a house" |
| 58 | 9 | (from bottom): "dialects, Dravidian" | "dialects of Dravidian" |
| „ | 4 | (from bottom): *Vījana* | *vījana* |
| „ | 3 | „ „ : Telegu | Telugu |
| 59 | 17 | "must be" ... | "may be" |
| 64 | 24 | Tosala-Otkala ... | Tosal-Otkala |
| 65 | 1 | Āvaśyaka ; -nijjutti | Āvaśyaka-nijjutti |

| *page* | *line* | *for* | | *read* |
|---|---|---|---|---|
| 65 | 12 | while presenting | ... | and presented |
| 66 | 4 | *βασι'λειον* | ... | *βασι'λε̃ιον* |
| „ | 12 | Athēna gounon | ... | Athēnagouron |
| 67 | 7 | Nondon | ... | Nardon |
| 68 | n. 1, 2 | Mihīra ... | ... | Mihira |
| 69 | 22 | Subhakaradeva | ... | Śubh° |
| 78 | 8 | Forchhamer | ... | Forchhammer |
| 82 | 1 | Mekalā ... | ... | Mekalāḥ |
| 90 | 8 | (from bottom): presents | | prescribes |
| 91 | 2 | the Muṇḍas the Santals | | The Mundas and the Santals |
| 94 | 9 | Amagabhutisa | ... | Amagha° |
| 97 | 5 | Mekal ... | ... | Mekala |
| „ | 7 | (from bottom): Vairāta | | Vairāṭa |
| „ | 9 | „ „ Kauśāmbi | | Kauśāmbī |
| 103 | 5 | up the Ganges | ... | up to the Ganges |
| 107 | 4 | *Carmadvīpaḥ* | ... | *°dvīpāḥ* |
| „ | 9 | Śulika ... | ... | Śūlikā |
| 120 | 8 | (from bottom): extends | | extend |
| „ | 9 | (from bottom): '*Kāmboja* (and not *Kamboja*) | | *Kamboja* (and not *Kāmboja*) |
| 122 | 12 | of n. 1, Insert | | before "the character" and "is read" after "which." |
| 123 | 13 | (from bottom): Kamtboja | | Kamboja |
| 124 | 9 | the Island of Palks | ... | Easter Island |
| 125 | last line | the best | ... | better. |

# INDEX

OF

SANSKRIT AND OTHER INDO-ARYAN WORDS TRACED TO THE AUSTRO-ASIATIC ORIGIN.

(*Words in italics belong to modern vernaculars.*)

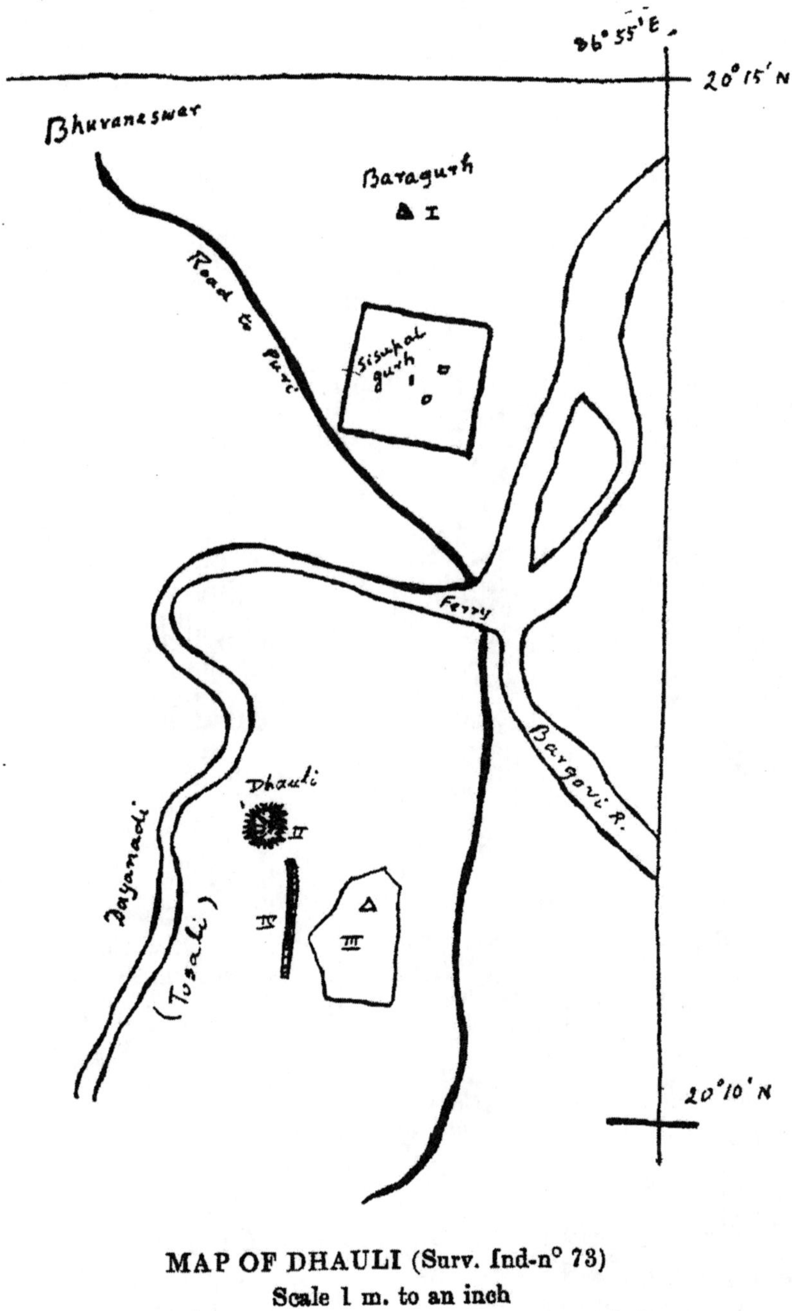


**MAP OF DHAULI** (Surv. Ind-n° 73)

**Scale 1 m. to an inch**

I. Pillar (Aśokan ?)

II. Aśokan Inscription

III. Kauśullá-gáng

IV. Embankment